IRRATIONALISM
AND RATIONALISM
IN RELIGION

IRRATIONALISM

AND RATIONALISM

IN RELIGION

By

ROBERT LEET

PATTERSON

GREENWOOD PRESS, PUBLISHERS
WESTPORT, CONNECTICUT

The Library of Congress has catalogued this publication as follows:

Library of Congress Cataloging in Publication Data

Patterson, Robert Leet.
    Irrationalism and rationalism in religion.

    Reprint of the ed. published by Duke University Press,
Durham, N. C.
    1. Religion--Philosophy.   I. Title.
[BL51.P32 1973]   201   73-436
ISBN 0-8371-6769-8

To

ARTHUR SLONE POHL

FOREWORD

I N THE THREE following chap-
ters I have discussed three fundamental alternative pre-
suppositions which determine respectively three points of
view from which the universe can be envisaged with a
view to estimating their validity by considering the consequences which follow from the adoption of each of them,
and also to evaluate their significance for the philosophy of
religion.   Were this a treatise in metaphysics, obviously
many of the topics touched upon with relative brevity
would require to be elaborated in far greater detail. What
I have attempted was merely to sketch in outline a position which I hope further to develop—or, if need be, to
revise—in the future.

I wish to express my gratitude to my colleague, Professor Glenn R. Negley, for reading the typescript of this
book, for proposing extremely helpful comments thereon
—which, as a matter of fact, resulted in the rearrangement
of the final chapter—and for most efficient aid in the matter of publication. I wish also to thank Professor Edward
D. Myers of Washington and Lee University for similar
friendly service with respect to the first two chapters, and
for equally appreciated advice in regard to them.

May, 1954, Durham, N. C.   R.L.P.

CONTENTS

IRRATIONALISM
AND RATIONALISM
IN RELIGION

IRRATIONALISM

THROUGHOUT the Protestant world during the nineteenth century, rationalism, as everyone knows, was predominant both in philosophy and theology; in the twentieth century the battle has gone the other way, and rationalism has been well-nigh driven from the field. In the domains of theology and the philosophy of religion faith has been exalted against reason, the "theology of crisis" has not only found a host of supporters, but has also inspired many who are not fully prepared to join its ranks to engage in individual onslaughts upon the rationalistic position. Coincident with these developments has been the growth of an evolutionary naturalism which professes to reduce mind to a status of cosmic insignificance, and the rise of a logical positivism which boasts that it has given the death blow to metaphysical speculation. Hostility to rationalism is the motive which all these various movements share in common.

An enlightened psychologist might find it worth his while to delve into the origins of a motive which has inspired such extensive and such discordant developments; the philosopher's business is not to impugn his opponents' motives, but to refute their arguments. Prejudices, conscious and subconscious—the latter, of course, by far the more insidious and deadly—are weaknesses from which every thinker worth his salt struggles to free himself. Value-judgments, indeed, are ultimate, and when these conflict such discrepancies must be noted; yet, when argument is impossible, it is a waste of time, and also a breach of courtesy, to fulminate against those who differ from us. Still it may not be amiss for one who adheres to the rationalistic tradition to inquire what weaknesses, real or apparent, had become discernible within rationalism itself which could have stimulated so general a revolt against it.

Certain facts are, of course, so obvious as to require merely to be called to our attention. Throughout the earlier portion of the nineteenth century rationalism was, to all intents and purposes, identified with Hegelianism. No serious attempt was made to revive the older forms of rationalism upon which Kant believed himself to have inflicted mortal wounds. And Hegelianism, after its initial and spectacular triumph which gave it all but entire possession of the field, speedily dissociated itself into a right and a left wing, and between these kindred schools civil war at once broke out.

> The trenchant blade, Toledo trusty,
> For want of fighting was grown rusty
> And ate into itself for lack
> Of somebody to hew and hack.

The birth of the Marxian movement in the household of the Hegelian left was probably an event of greater political than philosophical importance. What was of more intellectual significance was the fact that a sustained and critical examination of the Hegelian dialectic led a number of younger but extremely distinguished thinkers to repudiate the very method which constituted the common heritage of their elder contemporaries, with the result that philosophic anarchy ensued. If we wished to express ourselves in terms of a metaphor derived from the writings of Professor Toynbee, we might say that the dissolution of the Hegelian universal state was succeeded by an heroic age in which philosophic chieftains fought each for his own hand, while war bands, composed of thinkers whom the Hegelians no doubt regarded as representing the philosophic external proletariat, began to make incursions into the disputed territory. To put it in more prosaic as well as more exact language, the deep and far-reaching disagreements between singularists and personalists, theists and nontheists, in the rationalistic camp gave rise to a widespread impression that there was something very wrong with a way of thinking which generated so much discord.

We find this consideration urged with great emphasis by Lord Russell in his Lowell Lectures. Now the growth of naturalism was closely connected with the rise of the new realism, and new realism in its first inception confronted the world with a manifesto which exhibited an impressive uniformity of opinion among its protagonists.

The belief, moreover, was popularly entertained that the claims of rationalism were exaggerated, and that its performance by no means equaled its pretensions. The rationalists had been too prone to assume that idealism was the only form of metaphysics deserving of serious consideration and to dismiss the claims of realism as not worth discussing. The truism that every object—in the sense of an entity apprehended—implies a subject had been generally confused with the by no means self-evident assertion that no entity discoverable in sense-experience can exist unperceived. The unraveling of this confusion by Professor G. E. Moore and other thinkers led to a serious defection. By a natural reaction from one extreme to the other many were induced to conclude that mind, so far from contributing everything, contributed nothing, and that its role must be reduced to that of a mere spectator of a universe in which it existed only upon tolerance.

In the theological world liberalism and rationalism had hitherto been uniformly associated, the former being the offspring of the latter; consequently, the retreat of rationalism was bound to affect the status of liberalism. Some liberals, indeed, transferred their allegiance to pragmatism, which, under the leadership of William James, had frequently shown itself friendly to religion. The further developments of pragmatism, however, tended generally in the direction of naturalism, hence this position became increasingly difficult to maintain. When beliefs are valued only for their utility, the most obvious test of this utility will be found in the realm of sense-experience; hence, interest becomes concentrated upon the physical, and belief is pushed into the background as unimportant. Yet it is obvious that, if religious beliefs be true, they are important; consequently, the next step is to dismiss them as untrue. Thus naturalism, under the title of the new humanism, began to invade the theological world. Recoiling before this advance, many convinced religionists heard with relief the "drums and tramplings" of the cohorts of Barthian "neosupernaturalism" and hastened to join their ranks.

Rationalism is thus attacked both from the secular and the religious angles and is compelled to defend itself upon two fronts. If it is to survive, it will undoubtedly be compelled to renovate its entire position. But, before we scrutinize its capacities for so doing, let us attempt to estimate the actual strength of its several opponents.

To accomplish this we had best begin with naturalism; for naturalism is perhaps the most formidable opponent of rationalism, and one may suspect that, were it to collapse, neosupernaturalism would do likewise. Naturalism is, of course, a broad term which covers many divergences of opinion. It is sometimes used in so wide a sense as to be practically equivalent to empiricism. I shall not, however, so employ it in the present connection, inasmuch as there is a genuinely religious type of empiricism which it will be more convenient to discuss when we begin to examine in detail the position and the assets of rationalism. Nor do I think that this is the sense in which the term is most frequently used. The phrase "emergent evolution," so constantly employed by the most eminent spokesmen of the movement, is that which seems to offer the best clue to interpretation.

The naturalist's universe is an evolving universe. The fundamental concept is that of process, becoming. Reality is a series of events, a succession of states, a sequence of happenings. Not all naturalists would repudiate the notion of substance—indeed the late Professor Alexander, the most systematic and perhaps the most eminent of naturalists, deliberately employs it; yet substances, if they exist, are produced by and lapse again into the stream of becoming. They are, so to speak, merely prolonged events. The becoming, the process, is ultimate, and with it, of course, time. Behind these there is nothing. Probably the majority of naturalists would reject the notion of substance; and, indeed, it seems clear that the logical conclusion of this way of thinking is a doctrine of pure momentariness—the conception of reality as a succession of instants, each with its coincident happenings.

In this process, however, there is development. New and higher types of reality appear, supervening upon and supported by the older and lower. The term "emergence" has been coined to designate the origination of such novelties. It is intended to indicate that these are in no sense compounded out of, or reducible to, realities of a prior type. The stream of becoming flows upward. Reality is growing, not only in the temporal dimension, but also in richness of content. There is no working out here of any prearranged plan, no fulfilling of the design of a creative intelligence. The novelties are unpredictable; they are not implied by anything which went before, yet they presuppose what went before, inasmuch as it is the presence of the lower which makes the appearance of the higher possible.

Thus physical reality preceded the origination of life, and provided the environment without which such origination could not have occurred. Later, life subdivided into the vegetable and animal kingdoms; it was the presence of plants which rendered possible the emergence of animals, since it is obvious that these could not feed entirely on each other. Upon animal instinct supervened human intelligence, again a genuine advance, presupposing the previous stages of evolution yet irreducible to them.

The actual chronological order of occurrences is thus interpreted by the naturalist as involving a process of ontological development or "growth," as it is sometimes called. This is rendered feasible only by his acceptance of the Humean critique of causality. So long as causality was thought to involve necessary connection, the antecedent stages were perforce thought of as logically implying the subsequent states; which meant that the latter were reducible to the former, and thus, in a sense, contained within them. This led almost inevitably to the notion of a scheme envisaged in advance by a creative mind. Here was the difficulty which the old materialist, who maintained that atoms and motion could really account for everything, found insuperable. Mind ought to be explicable in terms of matter and motion, but, since he could not so explain it, he tried to revenge himself upon it by denying it all efficacy; yet it still remained an annoying reality which he sought to apologize for by such analogies as the shadow cast by the moving wheel. The contemporary naturalist makes merry at the crudities of his predecessor. He does not seek to account for mind, or for anything else, in terms of necessary connection. The beauty of emergents is that they simply emerge; unpredictable and unanticipated, there they are!

What is to come next? The superman? So some naturalists devoutly hope. Why should we assume that the process of emergent evolution has reached its goal? Why assume that there is any goal, or any assignable limit? Here we touch upon a point whereon there is some divergence of opinion. Lord Russell, who is certainly in sympathy with the naturalistic position, has thrown cold water upon optimism of a cosmic scope; and doubtless there are other naturalists who would agree with him. Many naturalists, on the other hand, would follow the lead of Alexander. The universe, they would urge, constitutes some sort of unity. There is no ground for the

assumption that the process of emergent evolution which
has taken place on this planet is not the manifestation of a
tendency which is operative throughout the entire cosmos,
nor is there any reason to suppose that in this particular
case it has yet exhausted itself.   There is no justification
for pessimism; therefore, like Mrs. Aleshine, we should
do well to embrace the optimistic hypothesis.

As regards theories of sense-perception, all naturalists
are, of course, realists of one school or another.   With
respect to the problem of universals it would be true, I
believe, to assert that the majority adopt either the position of the nominalists or that of the conceptualists.   The
powerful influence of Alexander does, indeed, support the
realistic hypothesis, and so does that of Santayana; yet
there is a certain inconsistency in such an attitude which
leads many, if not most, naturalists to draw back.   If universals be only mental constructs under which similar
particulars may be subsumed—a sort of intellectual short-
hand device, as it were—or if there be no universals at all,
but only particular apprehensions of particular objects, any
of which may be allowed to stand for all others which
resemble it in any respect, as Berkeley taught, then the
notion of process may be extended to embrace the entire
universe; and this is obviously what the consistent naturalist will desire. For, once the objective reality of universals
has been conceded, we are confronted by a province of
reality to which the concept of process is clearly inapplica-
ble.   And this is still more the case if it be admitted that
universals subsist, not only in particulars, but also apart
from particulars, not merely *in re* but also *ante rem*.   Reality is thus divided into two realms, that of becoming and
that of being.   And the situation will be further aggravat-

ed if values be included among these objectified universals, for the realm of being will now be quite as interesting and significant as that of becoming, if not more so; and, as a consequence, there will be the perpetual danger, against which naturalism must stand always on guard, that it may be exalted as the only ultimate reality, and becoming may be reduced to mere appearance; hence the persistent efforts of many naturalists to explain moral judgments in terms of emotional reactions, and to trace the distinction between right and wrong back to a primitive desire for social approval and a desire to escape punishment for antisocial actions.

In this brief and perforce rough-and-ready sketch, I have tried to delineate what I take to be the salient characteristics of the popular naturalism which has become so vocal during the last half century. As we survey it as a whole, what can hardly fail to impress us most powerfully is the fact that it constitutes an attempt to correlate the findings of the sciences and, in terms of these, to provide a consistent account of the nature of reality. To stick as closely as possible to the facts and to make as little as possible in the way of assumption is its dominant principle. It is this which constitutes its peculiar strength or peculiar weakness, according to the point of view. But what should be our point of view? Many criticisms have been passed upon naturalism by antinaturalistic thinkers, and I propose now to review briefly what I believe to be the most telling considerations which can be urged against it with a view to estimating its ability to withstand them.

As we inspect the outlines of the system we cannot fail to observe that it is composed of very old and well-worn materials. The doctrine of momentariness, with its coincident repudiation of the concept of substance, was worked out with a thoroughness which claims our admiration by Buddhist metaphysicians over two thousand years ago, and the Humean critique of causality was anticipated by the ancient Greek skeptics whose arguments are preserved in the writings of Sextus Empiricus. Of course, this is nothing against naturalism. Every philosophical system is constructed out of the ruins of its predecessors; it is in terms of the general design that it must be judged. Now, the critic may urge, it is precisely this that we miss in the case of naturalism. There is no central and dominating idea; indeed, there are no ideas at all; ideas are replaced by facts. We are asked to contemplate a succession of events as though this constituted an explanation, whereas it is just this that requires to be explained.

To this objection, the naturalist rejoins that it is based upon a mere rationalistic prejudice. It assumes that for every occurrence there must be a sufficient reason. Were the universe rational, the demand would be justified; but, unfortunately for the critic, it is basically irrational. What confronts us is not an intelligible system or a rational design but a mass of brute facts.

The critic, however, may urge that this contention is scarcely consistent with the recognition of a process of development from lower to higher grades of reality upon which the naturalist lays so much stress. Here is an amazing fact which does not appear to be at all "brute"; rather it suggests the presence of purpose. By what authority are we forbidden so to interpret it? When the various orthodox churches bid us accept mysteries "above reason," they at least profess to speak in the name of Deity. The naturalists, however, can invoke no higher authority than their own. Consequently the critics may feel moved to reply, "Rome we know, and Geneva we know, but who are you?"

These challenges, and counterchallenges, it may be said, do not get us very far. The strength of naturalism lies in its claim to adhere to the scientific method. Will that claim be called in question, or that method repudiated? As to the soundness of the claim, the critic might suggest that it is the naturalistic philosopher and not the practical scientist who has advanced it. The theory that causality involves nothing more than contiguity and succession is a philosophic doctrine imposed upon, and not derived from, the findings of scientific investigators. Had it not been for the belief that the external world is composed of entities which are genuine *things* and that these things exert real efficacy upon, and necessitate changes in, each other, scientific investigation would never have been begun.[1] Take, for instance, as a simple illustration the yearly inundations of the Nile which so perplexed the ancients. They assumed that subsequent inquiry would reveal an event which not merely preceded but also explained every inundation; and they were right in their assumption. The frequently repeated statement that science tells only the "how," whereas philosophy gives the "why," puts the matter far too simply. Science also seeks a "why," not the ultimate "why"—for it does not press its inquiry to the ultimate—yet, so to speak, a relative "why"; that is, it professes not merely to record but also to account for.

The Humean view of causality, the "regularity view"

[1] Cf. A. C. Ewing, *Idealism* (London: Methuen & Co., Ltd., 1934), p. 176. The antiphenomenalist may also appeal to that "running fount of erudition," the late Emile Meyerson.

as Dr. Ewing has so appropriately christened it,[2] has recently been subjected to very severe and, in my opinion, a very destructive criticism. Professors Montague, Broad, and Blanshard, and Dr. Ewing have raked it fore and aft.[3] I do not propose to try to recapitulate all the considerations which these various thinkers have stated with such cogency and in such fulness of detail. It will suffice if I indicate the type of criticism which impresses me as so conclusive by briefly summarizing several of the principal arguments.

The belief that there is an intrinsic connection between cause and effect, so that the former actually accounts for the latter, is either true or false. If it be false, how did it arise? The question cannot be answered without involving the very theory which is rejected; for any relevant answer must take the form of an explanation which accounts for the origination of this belief. The phenomenalist is thus confronted with an ultimate, inexplicable, incredible fact. Furthermore, if causality involve nothing more than contiguity and succession, how is it that not only "average men," but also scientists and philosophers, habitually select one of two simultaneous and contiguous events in preference to the other as the "cause" of a subsequent event? Why, for instance, do we attribute the death of a decapitated person to the fall of the executioner's axe, rather than to the coincident sneeze of one of the bystanders? Again, if there be no intrinsic connection between cause and effect, memory becomes at once inexplicable and untrustworthy, and inference from the nature of the past to that of the

---

[2] *Ibid.*, p. 153.
[3] The most detailed, and the most damaging, of these attacks will be found in Dr. Ewing's *Idealism*, pp. 151-187.

future becomes groundless. The laws of nature become mere runs of luck, with an ensuing violation of the laws of chance which successive occurrences cause to mount at a rate exceeding that of compound interest. It must also be granted that desires do not really determine volitions, with the consequence that the human will must be regarded as completely undetermined and as functioning with unmotivated spontaneity. Likewise arguments, however cogent, never constrain the most rational mind to accept them; all that we can say is that the presentation of arguments is actually followed by states of acceptance in some minds and states of rejection in others; but that all such states are alike groundless and their occurrence fortuitous, with the result that all disputation will become utterly irrational, since bad arguments will stand on the same level as good ones.

If these contentions be sound, as I think they are, the regularity theory collapses and whatever theory be put in its place will certainly recognize the presence of an intrinsic connection between cause and effect. Thus the naturalist's attempt to employ "brute fact" as a sort of war club wherewith to bludgeon the rationalist into giving up his demand for intelligible explanation turns out to be a failure. The importance of this conclusion can hardly be overestimated, since it is precisely in consequence of its acceptance of the regularity view that naturalism has vaunted its superiority to the older materialism.

There are, however, further considerations which point in the same direction. Naturalists, as we have seen, frequently speak of reality as "growing." In the realm of biology the term is used to indicate that expansion of an organism which results from the incorporation and as-

similation of nutriment derived from the external environment. Reality, however, has no environment; hence it
cannot grow in the sense in which an organism grows.[4]
Consequently, to apply the term "growth" to a process of
emergent evolution such as the naturalist posits is merely
to make use of a metaphor, and a misleading one at that.
If emergence as the naturalist has described it actually does
take place, it is in no sense the augmentation or expansion
of some previously existing reality; it is the origination of
something new, something which the universe did not
hitherto contain, an origination which cannot be accounted
for in terms of what preceded, an event inherently unpredictable and unintelligible, the most brutal of brute facts.
Growth, moreover, does not go on forever; it has its
natural limit. The organism reaches its ἀκμή, reproduces
its like, and a process of senescence subsequently ensues.
Clearly no similar processes can be attributed to reality
as a whole; if the optimistic type of naturalist be right,
the process of evolution has no assignable terminus.
The universe has not come to flower; beyond question it
has not reproduced its like. Once more, the notion of
growth is seen to be misleading if given a cosmic significance.

The notion of emergence is a special application of the
concept of becoming which, in occidental philosophy,
traces its ancestry back to Heraclitus. Carried to its logical
conclusion a philosophy of becoming involves the repudiation of the notion of substance, of a persistent particular
which can maintain its self-identity through change. Without the permanent, as Kant pointed out, there can be no

[4] See G. Dawes Hicks's *The Philosophical Bases of Theism* (London:
George Allen & Unwin, Ltd., 1937), pp. 185-187.

change; there can be only a succession of entities, each of which arises only to pass away. Thus there are no things, there are only processes; nothing exists, all becomes, occurs, or happens, whichever term one prefers. Thus the problem of apparent change is dealt with by denying its reality, by substituting for the notion of change that of succession, and by refusing to recognize the presence of any permanent factor. By so doing, Lord Russell has found himself enabled to solve Zeno's puzzle of the flying arrow.

The doctrine of momentariness thus possesses certain advantages, yet they are bought at a price. We have now to estimate whether that price be excessive. Consider, for instance, what happens to the self if such a theory be accepted. The self will now be reduced to a succession of occurrences of a psychical nature. All these occurrences will have this in common, that they belong to the same "stream of consciousness"—to use William James's famous phrase—but the identity will pertain to the stream, not to the occurrences. To state the situation in another way, the self consists of a succession of psychic states, none of which endures, but each of which arises and at once is gone, to be followed immediately by its successor. How, then, are we to account for what the plain man would regard as the persistent characteristics of a human being, for consistent integrity, for sustained resolution, for the ambition that is cherished throughout a lifetime, for affections that are maintained until the moment of dissolution? We can account for them only by attributing to the successive states similar characteristics.[5] But is not this persistent

---

[5] We must not say "the same characteristics," for this would imply the objective reality of universals.

repetition of such similar psychic phenomena a most extraordinary fact? To employ the notion of inheritance, as William James does, to describe this amazing reproduction by one state of the characteristics of its predecessor is to make use of a metaphor which neither illustrates nor explains. Nor is it open to the naturalist to invoke the connection of these evanescent psychic states with an enduring physical body as the basis of continuity, for matter as well as mind has been reduced to a sequence of events. We shall, of course, be given the inevitable naturalistic answer that becoming is simply ultimate, and neither requires nor admits of explanation. Yet this impressive continuity of pattern throughout the succession of psychic states powerfully suggests that this answer is inadequate; for it certainly does look *as if* there were an intrinsic connection between antecedent and subsequent states, as though the earlier states conditioned or necessitated the characteristics of their successors. To deny that such is the case is equivalent to asserting that this continuity, which is essential to personality, is the product of chance; and this, surely, is incredible.

If, however, the persistence of continuity throughout a process of inexplicable becoming be a difficulty for the naturalist, the emergence of novelty is no less so. For, if becoming be ultimate, will it not inevitably proceed in a haphazard manner? That subsequent events should occur as if they presupposed antecedent events, that the novel should supervene upon the familiar in such a fashion as to carry forward a steady process of development would seem to indicate the presence of some law, or some far-reaching design or rational scheme, which includes earlier and later events in its purview, and which provides either an enduring, or a nontemporal, basis for the entire process. Animal life apparently presupposes vegetable. But why should not things have occurred the other way about; why should not the animals have appeared first, only to die of starvation or to devour one another until none remained? Is our only answer to be that it might have happened so, but that, as a matter of fact, it did not?

Why, indeed, is the notion of emergence resorted to only in theory, and not appealed to in matters of scientific investigation or the conduct of daily life, as a sufficient answer which will render further inquiry superfluous? Let us suppose, for instance, that a ship founders in a well-charted sea. Were the rock on which she split a mere slender pinnacle, we might well assume that its existence had escaped the explorers of the ocean's surface. But let us again suppose that it is a reef of such dimensions as to rule such an explanation out of court. Were scientists, after due examination, to assure us that it was the product of an upheaval of the ocean's bottom as the result of a recently recorded earthquake or volcanic eruption, we should all accept the explanation without a murmur. Suppose, however, that we were told that the reef had simply "emerged," and that this was all there was to it. Should we not, one and all, scout such a statement as utterly monstrous? But why should we, if emergence be a fact, and a fact as ultimate and unpredictable as the naturalist says it is? Yet what would happen to scientific investigation, or to the carrying on of daily living, could such possibilities be seriously entertained? Would not painstaking search for remote and obscure "causes" be given its death blow? "Preposterous!" we reply. Quite so—yet it would seem to be incumbent upon the naturalist to indicate why it is that unpredictable and irreducible novelties emerge in so considerate a manner as not to disrupt the orderly process of events, and supervene so gracefully upon antecedent reality.

It may be urged, however, and, I believe, rightly urged, that these objections, pertinent though they are, do not go to the root of the matter. If the universe be basically irrational, if process be the ultimate reality, if pure becoming be a fact which we must simply accept "with natural piety," then anything can happen and nothing should astonish us. This is why a philosophy of becoming impresses the rationalist as absolutely preposterous. The laws of thought, he insists, are the laws of being. To assert that they are merely the laws of thought, and that reality may actually flout them, is to stultify the entire process of thinking at the outset, for thought is of reality. Professor Joseph's statement holds good.[6] To say that, while we cannot think of the same piece of paper as at once black and white all over, it may yet *be* at once black and white all over, is actually to affirm that we *can* so think of it, and thus to contradict ourselves. Reality, therefore, must be self-consistent; rational thinking is nothing else than the apprehension of its structure. It does not follow that much of reality is not unknown to us, it does not follow that there are not mysteries in nature in the sense of problems as yet unsolved; but it does follow that unintelligibility is always an indication that we have not yet penetrated to the ultimate reality, and that the progress of human knowledge consists simply in the extension of the process of penetration.

From this it also follows that the rejection of the

---

[6] H. W. B. Joseph, *An Introduction to Logic* (Oxford, 1925), p. 13.

scholastic maxim *ex nihilo nihil fit* is tantamount to a denial that the universe possesses an intelligible structure; for it involves the origination *in toto* and *de novo* of an entity whose appearance upon the scene is unimplied and un-necessitated by the universe as a whole. Nor can it owe its origin to itself, for, to bring itself into being, it must have existed while it was as yet nonexistent—a suggestion which is manifestly absurd. The intelligible structure of reality will thus be rent by the intrusion of a "brute fact," and therewith the intelligibility vanishes.

The attempt to treat process as ultimate, contends the rationalist, involves nothing less than the transformation of a relative into an absolute concept. For what is a process? In the view of "the man in the street" it is something that "goes on," but it cannot, he would insist, "go on" *in vacuo*. On the contrary, there must be a prior reality in which it "goes on"; it may consist in alterations in the nature of a single entity, or in interactions between two or more entities, plus the ensuing alterations in their respective natures; but such entities must pre-exist. More-over, some, at least, of these entities must be ultimate; whereas process is esentially relative. The playing of a tune, to take a familiar illustration, is a process; yet neither the instrument whereon it is played, nor the player who manipulates this instrument, is a process. To attempt to transform them into processes would be like treating the entities which produce an image—the sun and the water, or a man and a mirror—as themselves images. This way of thinking launches one upon an infinite regress which is plainly vicious. You can no more have process without a reality which is at least logically prior than you can have action without an actor. This, I think, is in substance what the average educated layman would say; and, in this instance, the rationalist is in cordial agreement with him.

Even were one to concede, however, that the notion of process may in general be treated as ultimate, there are peculiar difficulties in applying it to the self. And it is here, of course, that the naturalist is most anxious to apply it; for, otherwise, he will gravitate with alarming rapidity toward the position of Plato. Now, if the self be a process, or, to describe the situation more accurately, if there be no self, but only a series of successive and coincident psychic states—how are we to account for the fact that one can be directly aware of oneself? For that one can be so aware seems quite evident. I can be aware that I am aware of some external object, for instance. In this case, the subject which judges, "I am aware of an external object," identifies itself with the subject which is aware of the object.[7] Again, how are we to account for memory? How is it possible that I should recall an incident which took place years ago, and which in the intervening period has been totally forgotten? And how is it possible that I should identify myself with the subject of that experience? For the mental state which recalls the event is numerically other than the mental state which once experienced it, and between the two a vast number of other mental states are juxtaposed.[8] If, however, there be an abiding subject, a substantial self, these difficulties do not arise.

[7] This argument was first adumbrated by Lord Russell (see his *Mysticism and Logic*, New York: W. W. Norton, 1929, pp. 211-213; cf. the *Problems of Philosophy*, Oxford 1946, pp. 49-51) and subsequently rejected by him. It was, however, worked out in detail by McTaggart in his article on *Personality*, in *Hastings Encyclopedia of Religion and Ethics*, cf. his *Nature of Existence* (Cambridge, 1927), vol. II, chap. xxxvi, sec. 382, 386.

[8] This argument has been employed by McTaggart in the same connection (see his *Nature of Existence, loc. cit.*, sec. 389, 391), but it is also

The naturalist is not friendly to the notion of a substantial self, and for good reason. Processes can simply begin or end—as one can start and stop playing a tune—but substances, if there be substances, do not simply begin or cease. A substance can come into existence only by being compounded out of previously existing substances, and it can cease to exist only by being divided into its parts.[9] Consequently, if there be simple substances, or substances of which the parts cannot exist in isolation from the whole, such substances will be *sub specie temporis*, sempiternal; and entities of this sort will not fit into the naturalist's universe.

Even if we concede, however, that there is no self other than a mere stream of psychic states, the naturalist's difficulties will not be at an end. For most naturalists find it necessary to assume that later and higher levels of reality, while they supervene upon earlier and lower levels, do not modify the modes of behavior which were already habitual at those levels, and, consequently, that psychic states do not exert any influence upon the behavior of the brain or the physical organism. In other words, they are concerned to deny the theory of interaction.

It may be asked: Why, if he accept the regularity theory of causality, should the naturalist concern himself with this problem? If there be no intrinsic relation between cause and effect, no psychic state can ever necessitate the occurrence of any physical state; although it will also

---

to be found in William Ellery Channing's uncompleted and unpublished "Treatise on Man."

[9] If substance be defined as that which does not exist *in alio*, this statement will stand without qualification. If, however, we were to classify images as substances, on the ground that they have qualities and stand in relations, and are capable of persisting, the statement will hold true only of those substances which do not exist *in alio*.

be true, of course, that no psychic state ever necessitates the occurrence of another psychic state, and that no physical state ever necessitates the occurrence of another physical state, nor yet the occurrence of any psychic state. Since nothing ever necessitates the occurrence of anything, why disquiet oneself? I think that the objection is well taken. Yet despite the theory, just as he believes that the swing of the executioner's axe and not the coincident sneeze of the bystander is the cause of the decapitated criminal's death, so the naturalist appears to regard an antecedent physical event as the cause of a subsequent physical event in a sense in which an antecedent psychical event is not. Inasmuch as contiguity and succession are present in both cases, there appears to be no justification for this discrimination. Indeed, it would seem to imply a lurking belief that antecedent physical events can condition subsequent physical events in a sense in which it is important to show that antecedent psychic events cannot condition them.

Consider, however, what is involved by the denial of necessitation on the part of psychic states! It involves that, when a man goes to see his doctor, his awareness of physical discomfort and his determination to consult his physician have nothing to do with bringing him to the door of the doctor's office, that each stage of his body's progress must be explained wholly in terms of antecedent physical events, in the same way that one explains the successive stages of a rolling stone's descent from the top to the bottom of a hill. It follows that, when a man goes to the polls, his political convictions have nothing in the world to do with the way he votes. And it also follows that to try to foresee the future and plan against eventualities is futile, since no amount of thinking can affect bodily be-

havior.[10]   It is expecting a great deal of his powers of
faith to ask any man to accept such a theory.

Indeed, it seems quite obvious that no one would maintain a doctrine which, prima facie at least, is contradicted
by human experience during practically every hour of the
waking day, unless it were impossible for him to reject
it without endangering some cherished system.   What
need, may we ask, constrains the naturalist?   Granted that
mind is an emergent, having once emerged is it not as
real as matter, and why may it not interact therewith?
The answer appears to be twofold.   In the first place,
there is the law of the conservation of energy.   This so-
called "law" is, indeed, no more than a hypothesis, but
it is a hypothesis, the truth of which the physical scientist
finds it convenient to assume, and for the pronunciamentos
of the scientist the naturalist feels as much reverence as
does the Roman Catholic for a papal bull.   And in the
second place, although the emergence of novel and higher
levels of reality is asserted to be unpredictable and in no
sense to be implied by the antecedent and lower levels,
yet it is also assumed that these novelties *factually*, although not *logically*, presuppose, as it were, the reality of
these lower levels, that they build upon them, so to speak,
without in any way modifying their structure, much as a
higher story may be added to a house without disturbing
the lower stories.   Now, were it conceded that mind can
interact with matter, that psychical states can inhibit, alter,
direct, or in any way control the course of physical events
in the brain or body, the whole naturalistic outlook would
evidently become endangered.   Psychophysical dualism
would then become, to say the least, a highly plausible

[10] Ewing's *Idealism*, pp. 161-162.

hypothesis, and in its train appear other doctrines traditionally associated with it—the immortality of the self, the
existence of God, even a divine revelation—and it is with
a single eye to excluding these very theories that the whole
naturalistic philosophy has been developed; hence the
need to maintain that psychophysical interaction, which
the dualists take to be the most obvious of obvious facts,
is, after all, mere appearance.

The development of naturalism, as has been said, was
largely coincident with the rise of the new realism, and,
to a certain extent, the two movements overlapped. Idealism had made mind responsible for everything; the new
realism was determined to make it responsible for nothing.
It was to be reduced to the level of a mere spectator. Consciousness was to be explained either as a quality of the
physical organism, or as a relation subsisting between the
organism and some of the physical objects in its environment.   All this was, of course, congenial to naturalism.
But what was even more gratifying was the theory of
sense-perception elaborated by the new realism.   The
doctrine of representative perception was utterly repudiated.   The existence of the physical world was no longer
a matter of inference, for that world was now open to
direct inspection.   Although different individuals apprehended different aspects of the same object, yet the object
was as it appeared to be; it was possessed at once of primary
and of secondary qualities.   Though the stimulus emitted
by the physical object was received by the sense organs,
and, having been transmitted to the brain, induced consciousness to focus upon the object, yet no images were
thereby generated which could serve as a screen between
consciousness and the external world.   Consciousness was

not, so to speak, imprisoned in the brain; it was not compelled to trace in reverse the path of the incoming stimulus; without the interposition of any *tertium quid* it made contact, and direct contact, with its object. Knowing was an external relation which left the nature of its terms unaltered, hence a physical entity could function as an object of knowledge without its characteristics becoming modified thereby. The development of such a theory could not but be a tremendous boon to naturalism. As the theologian who is assured that the Deity is directly apprehensible is relieved of the need of demonstration, so the naturalist, being thus put in direct contact with the physical world, was obviated of the necessity of inferring its existence.

Such was the state of affairs some three or four decades ago. But times have indeed changed. Triumphant realism has suffered the same fate as did its predecessor— disruption and civil war. The realist had, indeed, undertaken a task which the fathers of modern philosophy, Hobbes and Descartes, had already esteemed an impossible one; he had determined to champion the position of the man in the street. But the man in the street is by no means consistent. In the matter of sense-perception he is doubtless as realistic as the most extreme realist could desire, but when it comes to dreams and hallucinations, he is a Berkeleyan of the Berkeleyans. Consistency, however, is the philosopher's mistress, and he dare not be unfaithful to her. Since images had been banished from the realm of waking life, they could not be permitted to intrude into the provinces of dream or fantasy; hence the extraordinary shifts to which realism was driven in the attempt to establish control over these areas; hence Alexander's amazing theory of the "squinting" mind, which relates the physical objects which it directly apprehends—without the aid of the sense-organs which it employs when awake—in another order than that in which they stand in objective reality, and so gives rise to the chaotic world of dreams. Although designed to support the position of extreme realism, this doctrine of Alexander's, be it remarked, actually modifies it, inasmuch as it assigns to mind something more than the role of a mere spectator, by ascribing to it the capacity to impose its own order upon the objects apprehended.

The rock upon which realism ultimately split, however, was the hoary problem of error in sense-perception. Lightly thrust aside at the outset, it was discovered by subsequent reflection to be more formidable than it had appeared to the first flush of enthusiasm. How, if the mind be directly aware of its object, can that object appear as it is not? The converging railroad tracks, the double candle flame, the elliptical penny, the color seen by the color-blind man, the straight stick bent in a pool, these, and numerous other entities, or pseudoentities, of the same ilk became perpetual sources of embarrassment. Despite numerous ingenious, and sometimes desperate, attempts to solve these various difficulties, an increasing number of realists became convinced that the original position was untenable, and that images must be reintroduced or, to describe the situation with more precision, that the reality of sense data, or sensa, must be conceded. Critical realism thus deliberately resorted to the theory of representative perception which had been championed by Hobbes, Descartes, and Locke.

Here was a schism of the first order within the fold of

realism. Some attempt to disguise its radical nature was, indeed, made by certain of the critical realists who insisted, rather disingenuously, that it is possible to "perceive" a physical object "through" corresponding sensa; but it was, of course, obvious to everybody that the term "perceive," when thus used, was intended to cover a process of inference, and that what was presumed to be directly apprehended by the subject consisted of nothing else than sensa. These sensa were, of course, conceived to be "private," not "public"; which is to say that no sensum could be apprehended by more than one subject. When the same object was said to be "perceived" by more than one observer, it was understood that there were as many sensa as there were perceivers. Moreover, inasmuch as visual and tactual data were not only private but also extended, it followed that there must be private spaces for them to be extended in. Each individual subject thus became the center of a little world of its own. That there was a common world with common objects in a common space remained, indeed, an article of faith; yet it was a world which was never directly apprehended by anybody. That this theory performs effectually the task for which it was designed—namely, to account for error—is evident. It was now the sensum, and not the penny, which was elliptical; there were not two candle flames but two images of one candle flame, and so on. But the most significant thing about it was the fact that the existence of a common physical world now became a matter of inference. The inference might or might not be valid; it could be, and it was, called in question. At best the existence of such a world could be no more than a probability.

So disturbing was this conclusion to many realists, who

were, nevertheless, convinced that the original thesis of extreme or naïve realism was untenable, that serious efforts were made to develop some other hypothesis which would account for error without invoking the notion of representative perception. The result was the rise of objective relativism. The root of the difficulty, we were now assured, was the simple-minded assumption that an entity must either possess a characteristic or not possess it. The relation between entity and characteristic was not dyadic, as had previously been assumed, but triadic—any entity possessed a characteristic only in a certain perspective or from a certain point of view. The same mountain might be at once green when viewed from a distance of five hundred yards and blue when viewed from a distance of five miles. Contradiction, it was affirmed, could arise only were the mountain to appear at once green and blue from the same standpoint. It was conceded by many that the emergence of such a characteristic might be due to the apprehension of some conscious observer; yet, it was maintained, the resultant characteristic, far from being a private sensum, was an actual and objective attribute of the physical object *in that perspective*. What the object was in itself and outside the various perspectives was an illegitimate question; for there was no outside—the object was merely the sum of its perspectives. Lord Russell, indeed, sought to stay the tendency to attribute such dangerous efficacy to mind by insisting that the plurality of appearances depended wholly upon the plurality of possible points of view, irrespective of whether or not these points of view were occupied by actual observers. The universe thus became a congeries of perspectives. The principal difficulty which confronted theories of this type—as Professor

Lovejoy has pointed out with such detail—was the consequence that common space became filled with objective
yet "wild" data which were incapable of interacting with
one another or with anything else, and of obeying the laws
of physical science.

I do not propose now to enter upon a critique of any
of these theories. What I wish to emphasize is merely the
effect of this epistemological chaos upon naturalism. For
the naturalist it is essential that some objective, nonmental
reality be posited as the point of departure of the whole
evolutionary process. So long as the epistemology of
naïve realism was generally accepted, the naturalist could
point to such a reality; the physical world lay spread out
before him and open to his immediate inspection. Today
naïve realism is on the defensive, and in the opinion of
many realists its case is a hopeless one. Yet, whatever
other theory of sense-perception the naturalist may adopt,
it will be one that will take him very far from the position
of the man in the street, and one that must be fought for
against numerous and keen-witted enemies.

Moreover, the developments of physical science have
dissolved the hard, indivisible, little atoms of the older
materialism into constellations of entities which seem to be
mere fields of energy, whatever "energy" may be. The
defection of eminent scientists, such as Eddington, to the
idealist camp is an indication of which way the wind blows.
Too much, it may be urged, has been made of all this. The
naturalist has himself been the first to stress the radical
nature of the difference between his view and that of classi-
cal materialism. Events, not atoms, are the ultimate constituents of his universe. But if the notion of event as an

ultimate unity be itself a mere metaphysical monster, his position is indeed in jeopardy.

Lastly, there is a further consideration which claims our attention. The new realism, as everybody knows, laid tremendous stress upon the objectivity of universals, and many naturalists were affected by this powerful influence. Thus Alexander, who was an eminent pioneer in the service of both causes, endeavored to include universals in his naturalistic universe by making them emerge at a definite stage in the evolutionary process proceeding from the primal reality, space-time.[11] But this was little more than giving them a mythological genealogy. Having emerged, they subsisted as fixed and changeless realities. This way of thinking results, of course, in a form of dualism—a dualism between the realms of being and becoming. And this dualism has, not unnaturally, rendered many naturalists uneasy; for their position would obviously be strengthened, could the entire universe be drawn within the realm of becoming. Hence of late years there appears to have been a drift in the direction of conceptualism and nominalism.

Neither of these theories, however, admits of being easily defended. Perhaps of the two views, conceptualism is clearly the weaker. For what is a concept? A mental product? But will it not, then, be as truly a particular as any mental state? When you cease to think of green, what happens to your concept? Does it lapse into nothingness? In what sense, then, when you again think of green, can you be said to entertain the same concept? Must there

---

[11] Primary qualities emerge in the initial stage of the evolutionary process; secondary qualities in the ensuing stage. The categories, however, do not emerge, but are included within the primal reality, space-time.

not be some continuity? Does the concept, when your
attention is diverted, sink into your subconcious, to be
fished up once more when you have need of it? How
then, is your concept related to mine? You form yours,
and I mine. Will there not inevitably be as many concepts as there are consciousnesses? And what have they in
common? If they all possess a common characteristic, we
are evidently confronted with a universal *in re* in which
they all share. Or will it be said that they are merely
similar? But this is to give the case away to the nomi-
nalist, for it is to treat similarity as an ultimate and un-
analyzable relation.

Nominalism is a theory which, at first glance, appears
so hardheaded and down-to-earth that it is almost sure to
exert an attraction upon the beginner in philosophy. Yet,
as soon as we try to deal with relations in terms of it, we
at once get into difficulties. If it be maintained, as it sometimes has been maintained, that a relation has no instances,
every relation becomes transformed into a giant particular
which pervades the universe—and what is this but a dis-
guised universal? It would seem, then, that we must concede that every instance of a relation is a unique particular
—as much so as the terms which it relates. But what now
are we to do with similarity? In no two instances will
similarity be an identical relation. There will be only similar similarities. An infinite regress will put an end to all
intelligible discourse. It is this consideration which has
recently led Lord Russell to avow his somewhat tentative
return to the realistic fold.[12]

If, however, we concede the reality of *universalia in re,*

[12] See *An Inquiry into Meaning and Truth* (London: George Allen &
Unwin, 1948), pp. 343-347.

to say nothing of *ante rem,* can we consistently deny the presence of values among them, as Lord Russell has always been inclined to do? Is not such a procedure arbitrary in the highest degree? Are not beauty and justice and courage obviously as truly universals as any other qualities? But if we admit the objectivity of values it seems clear that we are united to them by a relation which does not connect us with other universals. We feel the need to conserve and multiply instances of values. This is the relation which we term "obligation"; and it seems clear that it must be an internal relation—internal in Dr. Ewing's tenth sense,[13] in that it involves logical dependence. It does not, of course, immediately follow that values are the product of mind—indeed, I should contest any such assertion—but it does follow that mind and values are included in a logically coherent system. Without pursuing farther this train of reflection, we can see that it will conduct us to a metaphysical position profoundly different from that of naturalism.

The consistent naturalist, therefore, will deny the objectivity of values. And, with objectivity, obligation will vanish—for how can we be under obligation to what we have ourselves produced? The persistent effort to identify moral judgments with purely emotional reactions indicates the line which naturalism is bound to follow. A moral judgment will, then, possess the same kind of significance as a fondness for strawberries. The political repercussions of such a view are certain to be profound. An American naturalist may feel a personal predilection for a free state, but this will be his own individual whim. He has deprived himself of any ground upon which such a form of

---

[13] See his *Idealism,* pp. 136 and 183.

government can be philosophically defended. And in Nazi Germany and Bolshevist Russia we have seen how easily a naturalistic outlook can provide a foundation for tyranny. It does not, of course, follow that we are justified in dismissing a philosophy because we do not like its conclusions. But when a philosophy would make nonsense of moral judgments and the moral life, it is legitimate to demand that it furnish us with convincing proofs of the truth of its assertions. And it is clear that any arguments which naturalism can advance will be based upon a denial of the objectivity of values.

In the light of the criticisms which have been brought against it, we must, I think, conclude that naturalism has not made out its case. Despite the magnitude of its claims, its performance has not been impressive. Its fundamental contention that reality consists of a flux of brute facts, basically unintelligible, presupposes the acceptance of the regularity view of causality—a view which criticism has shown to be untenable. If so much be admitted, the whole system falls. And, it may plausibly be urged, it falls even if this admission be not made. In other words, it may be argued that, if the regularity theory be false, naturalism concedes too little, whereas, if it be true, naturalism claims too much. For any philosophy which takes us beyond mere phenomenalism involves an interpretation of the data provided by sense-experience. The rationalist makes bold to attempt such an interpretation, inspired by his conviction that reality is rational. The naturalist objects that the assumption is illegitimate, but by so doing he debars himself from initiating a similar undertaking. What is sauce for the rationalistic goose is likewise sauce for the naturalistic gander. Yet the naturalist wants to believe in an external world which is objectively real, and which is there even when he is not observing it. But how is he to justify such an inference, for, by accepting the regularity view he has logically restricted himself to the sphere of phenomena. Thus, when the naturalist makes use of the term "event," it is clear that he should employ it in a purely descriptive sense, to indicate a succession of appearances. And yet it is plain that he frequently means by it something more than this, something which has qualities and stands in relations and is objectively real in its own right whether observed or unobserved. What, then, may we ask, is new event but old substance writ small? If the regularity view be sound, clearly phenomenalism is the inescapable consequence.

Even if we waive this fundamental consideration, however, it is by no means clear that the naturalistic hypothesis enjoys any advantages when contrasted with such rival theories as theistic dualism or idealism. Creation may be an unintelligible notion, yet the naturalist is the last man in the world who should object to it on this ground, and it is certainly no more so than is the notion of emergence. Again the notions of a growing reality, and of the inefficacy of psychic states, appear to be involved in insuperable difficulties. In the field of sense-perception, moreover, there is no one of the conflicting theories the adoption of which decisively favors the contentions of naturalism—not even the epistemological monism elaborated by naïve realism, which is equally compatible with metaphysical dualism. We have seen the crucial nature of the difficulties involved in a rejection of a realistic theory of universals, yet the acceptance of this theory carried with it the recognition of a realm of a priori knowledge which is incompatible with the purely empirical approach so dear to naturalism. The denial of the objectivity of universals, including the objectivity of values, appears strangely inconsistent with the realistic outlook of naturalism in the field of sense-perception, and seems to many an explaining away of one of the most indubitable facts in the realm of human knowledge.

If these strictures be sound, their significance for the philosophy of religion is clearly maximal. For the obvious and avowed intent of the naturalist has been to develop a theory which will invalidate the claims of religion. It is true that the words *God* and *religion* are employed by certain naturalists, but only after they have been subjected to a process of "reinterpretation" which completely empties them of their traditional meaning. The words alone have been retained; that for which they have stood has been eliminated. In so far as the motive has been a desire to induce a transfer of emotions from one type of thought to another radically opposed thereto, the attempt is obviously futile, for emotions cluster, not about words, but about the realities which they are supposed to designate. Thus, when the naturalist uses the word *God* to signify a *nisus* toward higher levels of reality, or the word *religion* to signify an ethicopolitical outlook, he tends merely to produce confusion of thought in the minds of unwary persons who do not realize what he is doing; and since clarity is eminently desirable in these matters, it is hard to see what justification can be given for a usage which smacks rather of propaganda than of philosophy. Were naturalism, indeed, a universally accepted view, there would be more to be said for such "reinterpretation"; but, inasmuch as there are vigorous systems of thought which continue to employ these terms in their traditional sense, the usage in question is the more to be deprecated.

Dismissing this topic—which, however, is not entirely an affair of terminology, since it has also its ethical aspect —as of subordinate importance, I repeat that the contentions of naturalism, could they be sustained, would compel us to regard religion, in the sense in which the word is habitually employed, not only by the man in the street, but also by anthropologists, historians, and theologians, as a delusion. It is, therefore, a fact of the greatest importance if the arguments advanced against naturalism justify us, as I believe they do, in rejecting it. If this conclusion be sound, the alternative which confronts us as philosophers would seem to be between the position of rationalism, on the one hand, and that of phenomenalism, on the other.[14] Now, as we are aware, there is a form of phenomenalism which today enjoys a high degree of popularity, and which is termed logical positivism. There is much in this way of thinking which reminds us of the ancient Greek skeptics, yet, when compared and contrasted with the skepticism of the ancients, logical positivism is found to be more subtle, if not more plausible.

The fundamental principle upon which Greek skepticism is based in that of ἰσοσθένεια[15] or equal force. To every λόγος or argument which can be advanced in favor of any metaphysical theory, a λόγος ἴσος, or argument of equal weight can, it is contended, always be opposed; no conclusion, therefore, can be drawn, hence the only possible

---

[14] I say, "as philosophers," for, if revelation—in the sense in which the neosupernaturalists conceive of it—be invoked, we pass beyond the limits of pure philosophy into the field of theology.

[15] ἰσοσθένεια is usually translated by the term *equipollence*.

attitude is that of suspension of judgment, ἐποχή . Now it would seem in advance to be extremely unlikely that, in the case of every metaphysical theory, the arguments *pro et contra* would always turn out to be equally cogent. To be sure, we could learn only by trying, and before we had tried, we should have to envisage the possibility, even if not the probability, that we would finally arrive at such a position. As a matter of fact, this is the position which Schweitzer has reached, although in his case it does not appear to have produced the ἀταραξία —calmness, tranquillity, peace of mind—which, the skeptics assure us, ensues, inasmuch as he has found it necessary to seek an "ethical solution." Moreover, be it remarked, it is upon a very similar position that the Barthians base their appeal to revelation.

Now there is a consideration which, one would think, should go far to destroy the ἀταραξία of the skeptic, and that is the possibility that a closer scrutiny of the conflicting arguments might disturb their equal balance, or that some new and hitherto unsuspected argument might be advanced to which no equally cogent counterargument could be developed. Suspension of judgment, therefore, must remain merely tentative; it would constitute only a psychological, and not a properly philosophical attitude. This, to some extent, the skeptics realized; hence the repeated assurances of Sextus Empiricus that they do not affirm the insolubility of any metaphysical problem, but merely deny that they have themselves found any solution.

This is obviously a precarious attitude for the skeptic to assume, since it is in danger of being upset at any moment. The modern logical positivist is less naïf. He proposes to guard himself against any such untoward eventuality by denying that statements of a metaphysical nature have any meaning at all. All knowledge, he asserts, is derived from sense-experience. Meaning he identifies with verification in terms of sense-experience; hence a statement not so verifiable is nonsense. And, since all statements which bear upon metaphysics are unverifiable in terms of sense-experience, they are all nonsense. It is, therefore, a waste of time to try to discuss them.

The consequence of all this is as complete a phenomenalism as can well be conceived. Not only is the self dissolved into a stream of conscious states, the physical object is likewise reduced to a mere succession of phenomena. To the plain man there would certainly seem to be a meaning in the assertion that my coat is now hanging in my closed cupboard. The logical positivist knows better. Since nobody can see through the closed door, the statement cannot be verified; consequently, it has no meaning—it is nonsense. The statement that, when I open the door, I will see my coat hanging there, can be verified; consequently, it has a meaning and is very good sense.

The logical consequences of these assertions aroused such general incredulity that even the logical positivists shrank from sustaining them. For now it became nonsense to make any statement as to the constitution of the earth at its center—whether it be gaseous, molten or solid—or as to the other side of the moon—even to assert that it has another side—inasmuch as none of these statements can be verified by sense-experience. Accordingly, the logical positivists deemed it wise to concede that, so long as it was possible to *imagine* what such verification would be like, even though it were actually impracticable, an assertion would still have meaning—a concession which left the ban upon all affirmations of a metaphysical import still in force.

It is doubtful, however, whether this concession removes the real difficulty. The assertion that it is meaningless to affirm that sense-objects exist when unperceived is hardly balanced by the further assertion that it is meaningless to affirm that they do not. If our concern be only with sense-objects *when perceived,* we are practically condemned to a presentationist point of view—to a Berkeleyanism without a Berkeley, as one might say. The difficulties which confront the subjective idealist will now confront us also and with even greater urgency. For the subjective idealist the sense-image does indeed lapse into nothingness when it is no longer sensed, but the subject remains, and the God who caused the subject to become aware of the sensum remains also. The image of a cat in a mirror disappears when the cat wanders away from before the mirror, yet so long as the cat and the mirror are conceded to be persisting entities we can account for the appearance of the image under certain conditions. But if the cat and the mirror be themselves reduced to the status of images, we are left at a loss. Now logical positivism gives us a world of appearances which are appearances of nothing. There are no permanent and interacting entities; at least we are forbidden to affirm that there are—which is much the same thing. The "laws" of science are, therefore, reduced to the status of purely empirical generalizations; deprived of logical necessitation or metaphysical efficacy of any kind, they may at any moment be confounded and refuted by appearances of a novel character. The practical consequences of such a view concern the scientist as much as they do the metaphysician.

There is, moreover, a further consequence which concerns everybody. If the contentions of the logical positivist be accepted, we must all become solipsists. The truth of this conclusion has, of course, been denied, but the denial is uttered in a very faint voice. All that we know of other people is what we can observe in sense-experience—namely, their behavior. To posit any unobservable psychic states as instigators of this behavior is wholly inadmissible. Furthermore, the bodies of these people must be reduced to collections of sensa; and concerning sensa, as we have already been told, it is meaningless to ask whether they exist when unsensed. This means that when my friend has walked into another room and shut the door it is nonsense to ask whether he is still in existence. Moreover, since other people are reducible to groups of sensa, it will be futile ever to argue, for how could one hope to convince a group of sensa? Furthermore, since a priori knowledge is to be reduced to conventions with regard to the ways in which words are to be used, it follows that when I say that a certain object cannot be simultaneously black and white all over, I am actually stating only how I propose to use the words *black* and *white* and affirming nothing at all as to the nature of objective reality.

It will have been observed, however, that the logical positivist tries to make good his case, not so much by argument as by definition; that is, he frames his definitions so as to embrace his conclusions. Thus the assertion that all knowledge is reducible to sense-experience is sheer dogmatism, pure, undistilled, and undiluted. It requires us to regard other persons as the Cartesians regarded animals, as though they were mere machines; it insists upon explaining away the obvious fact of self-awareness; and, by subjectifying values, it eliminates what is distinctive in moral and aesthetic judgments, and reduces them to the level of mere statements of individual preference. And if we ask why we should accept a dogma which is in direct conflict with many of the most indubitable facts of human experience, the answer is that there is no reason other than this, that the positivist has so laid it down. It is a case of αὐτὸς ἐφα. The same holds true with regard to the identification of meaning with verification in terms of sense-experience. What could be more arbitrary than this? The meaning of a proposition is what is understood when the sentence in which that proposition is stated is heard or read. The words *mean;* what is *meant* is the entity which those words are intended to signify, namely, the proposition itself. The proposition is the meaning. The verification of the proposition is something other—it is an event the occurrence of which renders evident the truth of the proposition. Yet no such occurrence, either actual or imagined, is necessary in order that the proposition be understood. Indeed, it is patently obvious that there are some propositions which cannot conceivably be verified and yet the meaning of which is quite clear. Take, for instance, the proposition that you and I both experience precisely similar sensations when we taste sugar. This is surely a perfectly intelligible proposition; yet it is plain that it cannot possibly be verified. That we both like or dislike sugar is no indication that we both experience the same taste.

Consistency thus constrains the logical positivist to profess an inability to understand which amazes. Thus he is fond of saying that the proposition "God exists" is nonsense. It is not nonsense to the man in the street, who finds no difficulty in conceiving of a superhuman intelligence. If he deceive himself, if actually some confusion of thought be involved in the idea of God, let the logical positivist show us what it is. He reverts, however, to his definition. Meaning *is* verification in terms of sense-experience; the existence of God cannot be so verified; therefore, the proposition "God exists" is meaningless. It is not meaningless, however, to anyone who refuses to accept his preposterous definition.

Again, if the logical positivist be right, no proposition concerning the psychic states of anyone else can have meaning, for he has no justification for believing in the reality of any such states. As we have seen, all that the logical positivist can know about other people is what his senses reveal—namely, their physical behavior. To all intents and purposes they are, for him, indistinguishable from automata. But, if I reject this view as absurd, it is clear that the proposition "My neighbor is offended" will have meaning for me, since I myself know what it is to be offended—and this even though I am unable to verify the proposition, nay even though the evidence of my senses be against it, if courtesy or prudence induce my neighbor to conceal his resentment.

Even were we to grant, however, that meaning is to be identified with verification, we should still be entitled to ask why such verification must be in terms of sense-experience. The only answer is that the logical positivist has so decreed. But his decree flies in the face of experience. For no proposition that has to do with introspection can be so verified. I may, indeed, infer from my own behavior the presence in myself of feelings hitherto undetected in introspection, yet this behavior does not itself constitute verification, it is only ground for inference; verification will consist in bringing the buried feelings into the light of introspective awareness. Again, if I be told that by listening often enough to the playing of a certain piece of music I can develop a liking for it, the truth of this assertion can be verified only by subsequent introspection; my physical behavior may be suggestive, yet it cannot constitute verification, either for myself, or for others—who cannot tell that my seeming manifestations of pleasure may not be affectation.

There is no reason, then, why we should accept the basic contentions of the logical positivist. They are neither self-evident nor confirmed by experience. They are dogmas and nothing more. If we inquire why such a theory as logical positivism should ever have been elaborated, the answer is that it constitutes a desperate attempt to impugn the legitimacy and necessity of metaphysical speculation. Yet that such an attempt should have been made is a fact of deep significance. Farfetched and incredible as are the contentions upon which it is founded, logical positivism is at once the newest and the most uncompromising form of phenomenalism; and phenomenalism, as we have seen, is the abyss into which naturalism must inevitably fall in its struggle to become self-consistent. And phenomenalism, as we have also seen, is doomed to become solipsism.

Is not this, one might interject, precisely the course which events might have been expected to take? Does not the attempt to show that the universe is irrational constitute an effort on the part of the mind to disqualify itself, to commit intellectual suicide? And has not the attempt been successful? This road, then, leads to disaster; salvation, therefore, must be in the opposite direction.

Plausible as this suggestion may sound, we must not acquiesce too hastily. Naturalism and logical positivism have trained their batteries upon metaphysics, and religion is metaphysical through and through. The silencing of those batteries, therefore, should—one might well anticipate—yield gratification to every religious man. Yet, as a matter of fact, we find that many theologians are as insistent as are the naturalist and the logical positivist upon the irrationality of the universe—or, at least, upon its seeming irrationality when contemplated by the human intelligence, however rational it may appear to the Deity or an archangel.

This, at first blush, may impress us as an astounding fact. What has religion, we may well inquire, to fear from reason? But our question has not been rightly put. It should have been phrased, What has orthodox Christianity to fear from reason? And the answer is: A great deal. For, unlike Judaism, Islam, and Zoroastrianism—the other great theistic religions—orthodox Christianity is a religion of mysteries. The central doctrines of the faith—the Trinity and the Incarnation—have repeatedly been declared to be impermeable by human reason—and the efforts of those theologians and philosophers who have sought to render them intelligible have not proved too successful. It has been found that the safest course is to remove them to a realm of faith from which reason is excluded. There doctrines are to be believed, not because their truth can be demonstrated, but because they have been revealed.

Christianity is not, of course, unique in claiming to

be a revealed religion; this characteristic it shares in common with the three other faiths just mentioned. And in the history of all these religions the same problem has inevitably arisen—the problem, namely, of the relation of reason to revelation. Clearly, there are three possible positions among which a choice must be made: (1) we may declare that reason and faith are co-ordinate authorities, (2) we may subordinate faith to reason, or (3) we may subordinate reason to faith.

To the eye of a superficial investigator the first of these proposals would appear to have much to commend it. Neither the divine nor the human factor is depreciated; each would seem to be accorded its due. Yet the difficulties which ensue are of so crucial a nature that most theologians have shrunk from taking this way out of their predicament. For suppose the two authorities to be in discord. What umpire could conceivably be invoked to adjudicate between them? Like the empire and the papacy in the Middle Ages, each is ultimate; yet their domains overlap. War to the knife between them will be the inevitable consequence. Shall we then make it an article of faith that our two authorities will never disagree, much as Alfarabi posited a fundamental agreement between Plato and Aristotle? But this is practically equivalent to asserting that revelation can always be made to support whatever conclusions we see reason to adopt; and the effort to make this assertion good may involve superhuman intellectual agility upon our part. We shall have become exegetes whose exegesis is hopelessly biased by our philosophical predilections. And, what is more, we shall unconsciously have drifted away from our moorings, and by thus bestowing upon reason a *de facto* predominance, have actually conceded everything to the advocates of the second proposed solution.

Why not, then, consciously make this position our own? Why not boldly affirm the supreme authority of reason? But what need have we now of revelation? If reason be competent by its own unallied efforts to attain the truth, does not revelation become otiose? We may, indeed, answer as Locke answered, that the function of revelation is merely to provide reason with data which it could not otherwise obtain, and to indicate conclusions which reason may subsequently substantiate. The reply is a plausible one, and we can see why it was welcomed with enthusiasm by the early Unitarians. But the orthodox can scarcely acquiesce without great embarrassment, for the mysteries of their faith will thereby be placed in jeopardy. These must either be demonstrable, and so cease to be mysteries and become absorbed in some philosophical system or they must be repudiated as irrational. But can they be demonstrated? The efforts hitherto made in this direction have not been encouraging. It is easy now to understand the attraction which the third position, with its assertion of the supremacy of faith, must exert upon the orthodox mind.

To this position neosupernaturalists, as, for want of a better term, we may call them, have rallied with enthusiasm. They welcome all that the naturalists and the logical positivists can say in disparagement of reason. And they also welcome all that the rationalist can urge against naturalism and logical positivism. They ask nothing better than to see philosophers engaged in a hopeless internecine conflict. For thereby philosophy, so they contend, is manifesting its own incompetence to deal successfully with the fundamental problems of cosmology and metaphysics, and thus making evident the need for a revelation which can step into the breach and repel the forces of skepticism.

The attempt to vindicate the claims of Christianity by philosophical arguments is, the neosupernaturalists assure us, at once futile, illegitimate, and unnecessary. It is futile because the history of philosophy shows that it cannot be done. It is illegitimate because the motive that inspires it is human pride. And it is unnecessary, since revelation has in fact been vouchsafed. In the age-old effort of philosophers to grasp the fundamental nature of reality the neosupernaturalist sees nothing sublime. On the contrary, he accounts it a blasphemous attempt to storm heaven. Philosophic speculation has proved a mere tower of Babel, and the resultant confusion of tongues is a well-deserved punishment inflicted upon human presumption. Let the mind cease from its restless inquiries and be still, that in this stillness it may hear the voice of God and abase itself in adoration.

What philosophers, according to the neosupernaturalist, have failed to recognize is the all-important fact that the human intellect has been so damaged by the Fall that it is incapable of grasping the nature of Deity. Was this Fall an actual event which occurred at some definite moment in time? The language of the neosupernaturalist leads us rather to infer that the doctrine of the Fall is a mythical presentation of the truth that man, as a finite and conditioned creature, can form no intelligible conception of the infinite and unconditioned source of his being. God is wholly other. He may be worshiped, but he cannot be thought.

Accordingly, the most impressive characteristic of neo-supernaturalism is the tremendous emphasis which it places upon the negative theology.   The loftiest concepts which the mind of man can form are pronounced totally inadequate when applied to the Deity; hence the scorn which is poured upon anthropomorphism, even upon the notion of a personal God which arises so naturally and inevitably in the mind of the naïf reader who peruses the pages of the New Testament.   All such concepts are ideas which must be destroyed.   The imagination, indeed, may form its pictures, and, in so far as the mind recognizes the purely mythical character of its performance, such activity is legitimate and commendable, for the subjective value of such picture making is by no means negligible.   Yet it is of vital importance that this subjectivity be never forgotten, and the products of the imagination be not taken for literal truth.

The similarity between this point of view and the position of the Pseudo-Dionysius the Areopagite is, of course, striking.   For Dionysius also the function of thought is largely mythical and pragmatic, hence the positive theology is treated by him as a propaedeutic to the negative.   It behooves man to think of God as worthily as he can; and he may more worthily be conceived as living than as not alive, as mind than as matter.   By such a course of reflection the soul is stimulated and elevated to a point where it may profitably enter upon the negative way, wherein it realizes that God is other than all that it may conceive, and thus it is led on until it enters the "cloud of unknowing," where, beyond all thought, it unites itself directly with the divine.   In so far as there is a difference, it is, perhaps, in the more subjective emphasis which is laid upon this last stage by the modern neosupernaturalist; it is not so much the direct contact with God as the transformation of man himself in the impartation of faith which is stressed. The attraction of such a point of view for a mind which, wearied with speculation, yearns for a practical solution of its difficulties and for an experimental basis for assurance is obvious.

There is, moreover, another and very different type of thought which has contributed to the formation of this outlook, and that is the philosophy of Kant. The notion of insoluble antinomies which are inevitably generated by the mind when it enters, or attempts to enter, the field of metaphysics, is one which has exerted great influence upon neosupernaturalism. Perhaps it would be as true, or even truer, to say that neosupernaturalism is the product of the Hegelian understanding divorced from the Hegelian reason. If the generation of antinomies be the final achievement of an intellect whose powers of synthesis have atrophied, or which never possessed such powers, the recourse to a nonintellectual and purely empirical way of escape will be inevitable. And it is not the monotonous ἀταραξία of the skeptic, but the transforming and vivifying experience of being caught up by a divine energy which neosupernaturalism professes to offer us.

We must now touch upon another aspect of orthodox Christianity which will help to explain the desire of so many theologians to exalt faith to a position of absolute supremacy. A purely philosophical and rationalistic approach to the problems of religion is almost bound to depreciate the importance of the historic. Religion, like art, being co-extensive with human life, will be evaluated as such, and, if validated at all, will be validated everywhere. The superiority of Christianity, if established at all, will probably be arrived at in Hegelian fashion by vindicating the claim that it is the *absolute religion;* that is, by treating it as the logical terminus of a development the antecedent stages of which are by no means devoid of worth in their own right. Its kinship with other religions will be stressed as much as the differences which distinguish it from them. And in the process there is considerable danger that Christianity itself will be transformed into something very unlike the orthodox conception of it, the emphasis being laid upon what is universal and eternal, and the temporal being regarded as of secondary importance.

Now, orthodox Christianity, more than any other religion, is indissolubly linked to certain historic, or presumably historic, events. It is not, I think, correct to affirm with Professor Brunner that in no other religion do we find the idea of an event which has taken place "once for all." Certainly the promulgation of the Mosaic law upon Mount Sinai and the revelations accorded to Zoroaster and to Mohammed were taken to be climactic and unrepeatable events. And in Islam we find the notion of the embodiment of the Logos, not in a man, but in a book, which is plainly an event of the same order. But the all-important event for orthodox Christianity is the Incarnation. Now, while we find the notion of an incarnation in certain other religions—in Hinduism, in Buddhism, in Babism, and in Bahaism—we also find it there associated with the idea of a succession of incarnations. And, while it is both confusion and exaggeration to say with Professor Brunner that what is repeatable never takes place at all— confusion, because any event is, as such, unrepeatable; and exaggeration, because *any* incarnation would be a fact of the highest importance—it is nevertheless true that in orthodox Christianity we do have the notion of a single, unique incarnation. Hence, for those who accept it, Christianity stands apart from and above all other religions. It is founded upon an occurrence which has unique characteristics, which throws into the shade all that went before it, and reduces all that comes after it to the nature of an anticlimax.

To say with the Barthians that the Incarnation constitutes the breaking through of the eternal into time is to use language which, if taken literally, is, of course, sheer nonsense, as much so as to say that rotundity has become triangularity. What is changeless obviously cannot be identified with what is transient. But disregarding such outbursts of pious enthusiasm, we must acknowledge that, if the Incarnation have actually taken place, it is an event of the highest significance. Yet it is an event which rational speculation is helpless to deal with. One can, indeed, make many suggestions which will all be intelligible enough; but, unfortunately they will all be heretical. To say that the consciousness of Jesus was identical with the divine consciousness, which animated the body of Jesus and spoke through his lips, would be to say what, if improbable, is yet understandable—but this is Patripassianism. To say that Jesus was a perfect and godlike man in whom the likeness of Deity was made manifest, is to say what the Adoptionists said, and to make of the Incarnation a mere metaphor. To say, with the Arians, that the soul of Jesus was superhuman yet an entity distinct from God, is again to utter an intelligible statement which is heretical. The doctrine of the Hypostatic Union requires us to believe that the human consciousness of Jesus and the consciousness of the second Person of the Trinity were somehow united—without being confounded—in a single personality.   The best defense of such a doctrine is clearly to assert the incapacity of reason to deal with it; and this is the course which the neosupernaturalists have wisely taken.

I do not propose to attempt to criticize the doctrine of the Incarnation; for with such criticisms everyone is thoroughly familiar.   They have been stated with unsurpassable clarity and vigor by Channing, and I do not think that they have ever been satisfactorily answered.   But with regard to the attitude of the neosupernaturalist toward human reason there is, I believe, more to be said.   The doctrine that man is created in the image of God, when first enunciated by the unknown Hebrew author of the first chapter of Genesis, was clearly intended to stress the kinship between man and Deity.   And it is in respect of his reason, that most distinctive and ennobling of human characteristics, that this kinship, one would naturally suppose, would be most manifest.   To one who really grasps this doctrine and assents thereto, the exercise of his reason will be a means of communion with God.   It will be a sacred activity; the reason will itself be, as it were, a mystical faculty.   Hence the assertion that human reason is incapable of knowing God will impress him as inherently blasphemous, as striking directly at the very roots of the religious life.

This is what is done by the doctrine of the Fall.   To assume that this doctrine as propounded by the neosupernaturalists has reference to an actual definite event in the past would be to take Hebrew mythology with a seriousness which can scarcely be expected of us. Yet a more sophisticated interpretation removes none of those characteristics for which the rationalist feels so profound a repugnance. The doctrine of the Fall, one gathers, is a mythological way of bringing home to us the melancholy fact that man is a sinner by reason of his very constitution. It is not because of what he has done, but because of what he is, that man is to be so classified. His sin is his finitude. The very limitations of his humanity, his creatureliness, his susceptibility to change, estrange him from God. Sin is thus a metaphysical rather than a moral concept.

This is, indeed, an extraordinary doctrine. If sin be thus a common attribute of all human beings, rooted in their very nature, it would seem that it can neither incur nor deserve moral condemnation; for to be finite is no more blameworthy than to be a grasshopper. It would be absurd to find fault with a grasshopper for not being an elephant; it would be even more absurd to reproach a man for not being a god. That man is a being subjected to constant and manifold temptations and endowed with limited powers of resistance, and thus in perpetual danger of succumbing, we are well aware; but it is one thing to call him a sinner when he has actually sinned, and another to call him a sinner because he is capable of sinning. For man is capable also of noble deeds, of self-sacrifice and heroism; yet one would not call him a saint or a hero until his deeds have actually merited such an appellation. There is no reason why this moral plasticity of man, if I may so term it, this potentiality to become either base or noble, should be equated with sin rather than with virtue. Moreover, to affirm that because of sin man has been deprived of the knowledge of God is to imply that this dire punish-

ment has been inflicted because of some universal offense
on the part of the human race. But what offense can humanity as a whole have committed other than being itself?
Is the creature, as such, abhorrent to the Creator? We see
clearly what lies behind this way of thinking. It is the
atrocious notion of inherited guilt, transmitted as disease
is transmitted, the consequence of a primal offense on the
part of the first parents of the entire human race. The
effort to transform the account of an imagined event which
was believed actually to have taken place into a metaphysical parable has not eased the situation. The naïveté
of childhood has vanished, and has been replaced by the
self-conscious awkwardness of intellectual immaturity, but
there is no increase of credibility.

Furthermore, punishment implies the existence of a
judge who inflicts the punishment, that is, of a personal
God. Yet the notion of a personal God is utterly incompatible with the acceptance of the *via negativa* and the
total rejection, even in the very attenuated form of the
analogia entis of the *via affirmativa* which characterizes
neosupernaturalism. God, we are told, is "wholly other,"
and it is clear that by this is meant that he is other, not
merely in a numerical but also in a qualitative sense. God
not only does not include man as the absolute may be said
to include its appearances; he is also completely unlike
man. Now men are persons; hence, if God be wholly
other, he cannot be a person; nor can he be a group of
persons. Monotheism and polytheism are thus alike excluded by the *via negativa*. A balder challenge to theism
has never been proffered.

For what is theism? Theism, if we use the word in
its historic significance, is, surely, the hypothesis that the

universe is under the control of a single, superhuman intelligence.[16] How did such a theory ever originate? In asking this question I do not mean to engage in a debate with Andrew Lang or Father Schmidt as to the antiquity of the high gods. What I have in mind is something very different. What were the considerations, I would inquire, which, once mankind had attained the level of rational reflection, sufficed to engender this hypothesis? Some of them, at least, are clearly revealed to us in the sacred literatures of various religions and in the writings of philosophers.

In the first place, there was the presence of order in the world. The repetitive succession of day and night, and of the seasons, and the regular movements of the heavenly bodies, impressed it upon the awareness of everyone. It was incredible that such order should be the offspring of chance, and the only other source to which it seemed plausible to ascribe it was design. In the second place, there were sporadic events, such as the occurrence of tempests, pestilences, etc., which to the mind of early man —who was no Humean positivist—required a sufficient reason; and where could such a reason be found except in a superhuman intelligence endowed with superhuman power? In the third place, there was the awareness—implicit, rather than explicit, no doubt, in the minds of the generality of men, yet none the less, real and potent—of the worth of life and mind. Indeed the notion of the inanimate, as the history of Greek philosophy makes clear

[16] Most theists have also believed that the supreme Intelligence has brought the universe into being, yet in this not all theists would concur; for some have held that matter, finite spirits, or universals—or all of these— are uncreated, and see in the divine Mind only the principal of order, or even—as in the case of Patanjali—only a Saviour.

to us, was formulated only at an advanced stage of reflection and called for a very considerable capacity for abstraction. The first clear statement of it which we possess is to be found in Plato's discussion of death in the *Phaedo,* and in all probability it was the experience of corpses from which the animating principle had departed which first suggested the possibility of the existence of entities permanently devoid of life. Once the antithesis between mind and matter had been definitely envisaged, it must have seemed to many philosophers, as it does to the Eleatic stranger in the *Sophist,* absurd to assume that ultimate reality should be deprived of life and mind. And in the fourth place, motion has always ranked high among "the criteria of livingness,"[17] and this fact, we know, suggested to Plato the line of argument which he developed in the *Phaedrus* and the *Laws,* directed to showing that all motion must be traced back to the soul as its original cause, and finally to a supreme soul as the principle of order. And, in the fifth place, all these considerations must have blended with, and been completely reinforced by, the thirst for communion with a power greater than, and yet akin to, man which is so characteristic of a certain type of mystical religion.

All these various types of reflection are plainly inspired by a single conviction, namely, that the universe can be understood in terms of mind. It is from his knowledge of himself that man develops his idea of God. Theism is anthropomorphic through and through. To say this is not to say anything against it. Anthropomorphism is "crude" —to use the adjective so often and so carelessly coupled

[17] The phrase is J. Arthur Thomson's. See *The System of Animate Nature* (London: Williams, 1920), Vol. I, Lecture III.

with it—only when man's conception of himself is crude.
Before mind and matter were abstractly viewed as distinct
and separate, man's outlook was roughly hylozoistic. The
souls of the dead had bodies of a sort, so did superhuman
spirits, so did the gods. When Yahweh summons Samuel,
he comes and stands and calls for him, as a man would
do.[18] With the development of a dualistic point of view,
the situation is altered. It is in respect of the vital principle within him, of his life, will, emotion and reason—as
we should say today, of his personality—that man resembles God. Such an anthropomorphism is no longer
crude; it is genuinely philosophical and metaphysical.
Whether the theistic hypothesis be sound or no is a matter
of debate, but that it constitutes one of the most magnificent constructive achievements of the human intellect is
indisputable. And it is evident that the theist who permits
himself to sneer at anthropomorphism is engaged in saw-
ing off the branch that he is sitting on.

Now this is precisely what the negative theology does.
If its contentions be justified, then the entire theistic hypothesis is illegitimate. If "God" be wholly other than
man, other not only in a numerical but also in a qualitative
sense, then "he" is not God at all in the sense in which the
theist understands the word. The personal pronoun will
be applied to him only in obedience to conventional usage.
The negative theology leads us straight to an impersonal
absolute, to the Unconditioned of certain contemporary
thinkers. Perhaps, you may say, it is none the worse for
that. May not theism in the long run prove to be philosophically indefensible? Perhaps it may. And are there
not such genuine nontheistic religions as Jainism and

[18] I Sam. 3:10.

Hinayana Buddhism? Indeed there are. But the negative theology will invalidate these also. For, although
these religions do not equate mind with ultimate reality,
they do nevertheless insist that all minds and all souls are
permanent constituents of ultimate reality. And this is a
groundless and unwarranted assertion if the contentions
of the negative theology be true. If we elect, then, to
follow the way of negation, it is plain where it will take us.
It will take us to the only form of religion which has ever
applied it wholeheartedly and consistently, namely, to Zen.

Here we arrive at a religious empiricism of the most
uncompromising type. Zen has no official philosophy nor
theology. Ultimate insight, it maintains, is the terminus,
not of philosophical, but of psychological, progress; it is
reached, not by discursive thought, but by concentration.
Accordingly, Zen devotes its attention to the technique of
mysticism. The attainment of *satori*—i.e., liberation—is
a practical, not a theoretical matter; moreover, the content
of that enlightenment cannot be communicated by one man
to another either by tongue or pen, for it is essentially
ineffable.

Such a position is obviously secure against direct intellectual attack; for, where no argument is advanced, refutation is impossible. The authority of the Zen master
reposes upon no dogmatic preconception; it is simply that
of an expert in the spiritual life. And, if we ask why we
should treat his claim seriously, we are told that others
who have followed his guidance have actually attained
enlightenment, and the challenge is proffered us to do
likewise.

Now this, I would urge, is the only position which the
irrationalist who is also a religionist can consistently oc-

cupy. Where dogma is advanced, the understanding is
appealed to; questions may be asked and must be answered; proof must be given or authority indicated—in
either case, discussion is inevitable and argument must be
resorted to. And, when reason has once been invoked, she
cannot be silenced until *some* concessions at least have been
made to her. But *any* concessions are fatal to the claims
of irrationalism. Zen, however, advances no dogmas and
thereby avoids the necessity of any concession. Its position
is that of pure, psychological empiricism.

Self-consistent, however, as this position is, there are
two important observations to be made in regard to it. In
the first place, it is utterly incompatible with any theory
of revelation. For revelation involves a revealer; it implies the intent to communicate some intelligible message,
and such an intention can be entertained only by an intelligence. Consequently, when the existence of a personal
God is denied, the notion of revelation becomes nonsense.
Now theism, as we have seen, is an attempt to interpret
the universe in terms of mind or reason. The notion of
revelation, therefore, is rationalistic through and through.
This is a fact which it behooves us to keep in mind, for the
assumption is frequently made that reason and revelation
must be at odds. This, however, is due to the historic accident that much of what claims to be revelation is incredible. The neosupernaturalist, saddled as he is with unintelligible "mysteries," finds it necessary to accept the assumption and consequently to decry reason. But this in
no way impugns the notion of revelation. I do not say
that rationalism must make a place for a doctrine of revelation; this is a problem yet to be investigated. All that I
assert is that the notion of revelation presupposes that the

universe is, to some extent at least, rational, and that, consequently, he who asserts that the universe is fundamentally irrational is logically compelled to reject the notion of revelation. This consideration, however, affects only the theist.

In the second place, we may seriously question whether the mystical enlightenment which is the goal of Zen is as entirely self-sufficient and independent of all processes of rational reflection as it asserted to be. Despite their official reticence, Zen mystics, like other mystics, find it impossible to maintain an unbroken silence, and what they tell us of their experience makes it clear, I think, that it is not merely emotional, but that it is also cognitive—or, at least, that they consider it to be cognitive. What might they become aware of that could be ineffable? The answer might well be, a new value. There is nothing inherently incredible in the suggestion. There must have been a time when moral values were first perceived by some man or group of men, even though it did not happen in the Garden of Eden after eating of the Tree of Knowledge. And the same holds true of aesthetic values. The experience of any value is, of course, ineffable. It cannot be described to one who has not shared it; and no argument can acquaint him who is ignorant of it with its nature, any more than argument can communicate to any man an awareness of the nature of a sense-datum which lies outside the field of his experience. Now the advocates of the doctrine of "the religious *a priori*" tell us that there are specifically religious values which can be subsumed under the category of the "holy" or the "sacred" of which one can thus become immediately aware. Is it possible that the experience of *satori* is productive of such an awareness, or that it at least makes clear an awareness which before was only confused? Let us concede so much. Still, all this is very vague. In what do these values inhere, or what do they characterize? We cannot at this time of day be expected to find them in stones and trees and springs which savages account sacred. Moreover, the experience of *satori* clearly has something to do with human destiny; it is described as removing illusion and bringing peace to the soul. A world view, then, is evidently involved; it is in the universe as a whole that value inheres; it is seen, as it were, from inside, as a whole; the principles of its structure are discerned in a synoptic vision.

This is a tremendous claim, yet it appears to be made. And, while we may hesitate to reject it as incredible, we may yet ask without impertinence whether in such a world view elements derived from antecedent philosophic speculation are not bound to be incorporated, albeit surreptitiously and without acknowledgement. And we may ask it all the more emphatically when we reflect how great a role the Lankavatara Sutra plays in the history of Zen, for the inspiration of this sutra by a metaphysical monism is evident beyond all cavil. I am not now asserting that mystical insight constitutes the natural culmination and the empirical corroboration of metaphysical construction, as so many philosophers since Plato have hoped and believed. I am only arguing that to any vision of cosmic breadth and depth, however intuitively arrived at, rational reflection will make its inevitable contribution; and that in a purely irrational universe the occurrence of any such experience would be inconceivable. If this much be admitted, the conclusion will hardly be contested that irrationalism, so far from being the friend of religion, is its inveterate enemy. Having arrived at this conviction, which is one of no mean significance, we may next proceed to examine the position of those who hold that the universe is neither wholly irrational, nor yet wholly rational, but partly rational and partly irrational.

CHAPTER II

IRRATIONALISM PLUS RATIONALISM

THE VIEW that the universe is neither a completely intelligible and perfectly ordered rational system nor yet at bottom a chaos of utter irrationality, but rather the product of two mutually independent principles—rationality and irrationality—is one which, at first glance, can scarcely fail to appear attractive. Indeed it appears to be empirically confirmed in human experience. If we say that the universe is basically irrational, how are we to account for the presence of law and order within it? Yet upon that presence not only the existence of science but human life itself is absolutely dependent. To attempt to account for the laws of nature as mere runs of luck is, as we have seen, a desperate expedient. To classify them as "emergents" is to resort to an explanation which does not explain, but is purely verbal. Moreover the laws of logic and of mathematics constitute a scheme in accordance with which *any* conceivable universe must be constructed. Clearly, then, they are *grounded* in the nature of ultimate reality. Yet, on the other hand, there appear to be obvious limits to the process of rationalization. Space and time—or, to be more up-to-date, space-time—matter, life-consciousness, sense-data—some, if not all, of these we must, it would seem, take as ultimate and irreducible. Yet reason is restive before arbitrary restraint; it demands that all these be reduced to some ultimate principle from which they can in turn be deduced a priori, so that the whole system will be rendered transparently intelligible—and is not this an impossible claim? Extensive as are the conquests of reason, impressive as are its undoubted and genuine achievements, is it not plain that there are limits which it cannot overpass, ultimate irrationalities which it must simply accept?

Again, does not such an attitude impress us as manifesting both a legitimate confidence and a becoming modesty? The irrationalist, having striven to shout down all his opponents, is apt to speak as though his own voice were the voice of revelation. The rationalist, with his tremendous claims, seems to aspire to "become Zeus." But the defender of the intermediate position appears to "speak forth the words of truth and soberness,"[1] to acknowledge all the inherent capacities and genuine achievements of reason, and to refuse to recognize only preposterous claims which cannot be made good.

Part of the universe, then, is rational in structure and therefore penetrable by the intellect, but beyond its boundaries lies, we are told, an obscure realm of utter unintelligibility. It is important to emphasize that, according to the theory now before us, this unintelligibility is not apparent but real. It is this contention which distinguishes the view in question from pure rationalism. For the rationalist does not deny the presence of *seeming* irrationality, but he maintains that it is seeming only. Nor

[1] Acts 26:25.

does the rationalist of today profess to account for the existence of any individual particular by a deductive method in the way that Hegel claimed to demonstrate the necessary existence of seven planets. All that the rationalist asserts is that reality constitutes a rational system, and that the human intellect by virtue of its inherent rationality is capable of grasping, to some extent at least, the nature of that system. He is not concerned to deny that every unsolved problem confronts us with an apparent irrationality, but he points out that it is the conviction that such irrationality is appearance only and that the reality behind it is rational which has encouraged the scientist to solve problem after problem and to advance from achievement to achievement. It is true that the solution of one problem frequently generates another and that the apparently irrational in the sense of the as-yet-unsolved mystery perpetually flits before us, yet this does not disturb the firmness of the conviction, nor need the rationalist deny that there may be problems which, because of man's inherent limitations, because of his location on this particular planet, for instance, and the restricted range of his sense organs and scientific instruments, will remain permanently insoluble. He is not committed, for example, to the assertion that we shall one day be able to describe the contour of the other side of the moon. What he is committed to is the affirmation that what is unknown is in itself intelligible.

Moreover it is to be observed that, in maintaining that some of the characteristics of ultimate reality can be grasped by the human mind, the rationalist is in agreement with the defender of the intermediate position. What the latter contends is that ultimate reality is not wholly intelligible, that there is a realm which is irrational *in se*.

And by this contention he commits himself to some form of *ontological* dualism. The question then arises: How is this ultimate dualism to be envisaged?

Are we to think of the irrational principle as antirational in the sense of being in positive opposition to the rational, or merely as nonrational in the sense of a negative principle, a sort of dead weight which inhibits the activity of the rational? The former suggestion would seem to imply something *demonic* in character, irrationality in the sense of wickedness. If it be urged that this would constitute a futile attempt to rationalize the irrational, to render intelligible the inherently unintelligible, it might be answered that the supremely irrational is the will which subordinates reason to its perverted and frantic desire, as the cleverness of an evil man may exhibit incredible subtlety and ingenuity in the pursuit of a pernicious and destructive purpose. Whether Plato actually intended to embrace this hypothesis in the tenth book of the *Laws* is a matter of dispute, as is also the ultimacy of Zoroaster's dualism; but one can very well understand why this theory, in its unqualified form, has attracted relatively few philosophers or religionists. If the universe be sundered into two opposing camps each under the leadership of a single conscious intelligence—one morally perfect and the other completely wicked—it seems clear that the final victory of either party will be impossible; for the strife between them will have endured throughout a limitless past wherein every possibility will have been already actualized. Should it be urged that, if the past be conceived as finite, this objection falls, the point must at once be conceded; yet, so far as I know, the only theorists who have posited an absolute beginning have been either evo-

lutionary naturalists, who would scout the notion which
we are now considering as mere mythology, or scholastics
who were ready enough to acknowledge the existence of a
devil, but who insisted that he is a created, and therefore
a subordinate power. The objection also falls, it is true,
if time be treated as mere appearance; but those thinkers
who have so treated it have all been monists of one sort or
another for whom the notion of an ultimate and absolute
dualism was inadmissible. For these various reasons
philosophers have been disinclined to favor the theory.
Religionists also find it unwelcome, for one of the most
salient characteristics of religion, especially in its more
advanced forms, is its invincible optimism which renders
the notion of interminable conflict between good and evil
uncongenial.

Moreover, on empirical grounds, the view in question
would find little to commend it. Only the most extreme
and indurate monist, indeed, would be prepared to deny
the reality of evil; and once that reality be admitted, no
very acute observation is needed to determine that upon
this planet both its extent and intensity are appalling.
Nevertheless, as Professor Toynbee has reminded us in so
impressive a fashion, the time that has elapsed since the
birth of the first civilizations is short indeed compared with
the period during which man has been an inhabitant of
this planet, and yet, despite the occurrence of dark ages
and periods of disintegration and decay, the progress
achieved during this relatively tiny span has been simply
amazing. Notwithstanding their ceaseless activity, the
temporary triumphs of the forces of evil are seen, when a
long view is taken, to constitute only Pyrrhic victories
which cover a clearly perceptible, if by no means continu-

ous, retreat. Granted that this process may conceivably be reversed in the future, there seems no justification for regarding this abstract possibility as a probability. The situation which confronts us, therefore, is not such as we should expect to find if the hypothesis before us were a sound one, and we may, therefore, make bold to dismiss it.

How, then, is the inescapable dualism to be conceived? Shall we posit an ultimate and irreducible distinction between life or mind, on the one hand, and matter on the other, and envisage the former as inserting itself into and utilizing a stuff essentially alien to it? Bergson has at times written as though he accepted some such theory, although, as we know, this was not his final view, and perhaps never was for him more than a provisional hypothesis. But how are we to conceive of matter, which our scientists have rendered so evanescent? The solid little particles which were the delight of the materialists of former ages have been eliminated. Shall we substitute the notion of energy? But what is energy in itself, if it be something other than modes of behavior? To this question it is difficult, if not impossible, to return a definite answer. The tendency seems to be to replace the notion of matter by that of event, but, if I have been right in arguing that the notion of event is itself relative, it is clear that here there is no ultimate refuge. Shall we, then, embrace the suggestion offered by Plato in the *Timaeus* and posit space and motion as ultimate? Alas, space and motion have both been pronounced relative, and consequently refer us to something beyond themselves. Moreover, the failure of the new realism to make good its epistemological contentions raises the problem of private spaces which certainly seem to be required by private sensa, and these in turn necessitate our asking how they are to be related to public space, and whether public space be, after all, anything more than an intellectual construct developed to aid us in correlating private spaces. One thing, at least, is obvious in the light of these reflections. If there be an objective, physical world, its existence and its nature can be definitely established only by a complicated process of epistomological and metaphysical inquiry which has not as yet been carried to a successful conclusion.

There is, however, another form of dualism the recognition of which may prove welcome to the defender of the intermediate position. It is that of the universal and the particular. In the realm of universals thought is traditionally at home. Here it deals with the intelligible and the eternal. But when it turns to particulars it passes from the transparent to the qpaque; it seems to enter the domain of the arbitrary and the unintelligible. Is there anything, we ask, in the nature of the universal to compel it to characterize any particulars at all? Is the notion of a universal which has no instances untenable? What of perfect virtue, for instance? Can we not conceive of it? Yet, having done so, are we constrained to posit a particular which it characterizes—and, if so, only one particular, or more than one? Of the universal, Cook Wilson has affirmed with admirable succinctness and lucidity: "It is not necessary that it should be in more than one, and its nature is not constituted by being in a plurality. It is what it is not because it is in a plurality; it can be in a plurality because it is what it is."[2]

Why, then, should not reality be constituted exclusively of universals? Why should there be any particulars at

2 *Statement and Inference* (Oxford, 1926), II, 711.

all? That there actually are particulars is a fact which brooks no denial. The nature of any particular is, indeed, composed of universals; yet, if we try to treat particulars as nothing more than "bundles" or "cross sections" or "togethernesses" of universals, we are nonetheless forced to admit that *this* togetherness is distinct from, and numerically other than, *that* togetherness—in other words, that it is a particular togetherness. Why should this be so? If the number of particulars in the universe be infinite, why infinite?—if finite, why this number rather than some other?

To use a homely simile, universals are like clotheslines, and particulars are like the props that support them. The number of props, as well as the number of lines, will be dictated by the general design. And that design will subsist, apart from the props and the lines, in the consciousness of the designer who arranged them. Was it some such reflection as this which led the mature Plato to posit a divine mind as "the cause of the mixture?" No doubt it was. Shall we follow his example? And, if we do so, shall we succeed in exorcizing the specter of the irrational? So long as, with Plato, we retain some ultimate, nonmental reality, such as space, so long will we still be confronted with brute fact. Is it not clear that a rational universe must be a mental universe? Must we not, therefore, see in the Deity a creative source whence universals and particulars alike proceed? Neoscholastic writers are never tired of affirming that the doctrine of creation possesses a philosophic value of the highest order, and now we see what the basis of their contention is. It is only thus, they believe, that brute fact can be eliminated and the rationality of the universe vindicated.

It behooves us, therefore, to examine the doctrine of creation. It is one with which we are so thoroughly familiar that it is not easy for us to realize how startling it must appear to one previously unacquainted with it. And this familiarity is doubtless reinforced by the frequent confusion of the notion of creation with that of making. Our first duty, accordingly, is to distinguish between them. To make is to utilize some material already existing, and to adapt it to our own purposes. In Aristotelian language it is to impose a new form upon pre-existing matter. Creation, on the other hand, is "out of nothing." This famous phrase does not mean that nothing or nonbeing is the matter out of which something is produced. On the contrary, it means that the new entity is not produced out of anything, that it is brought into being *in toto* and *de novo*. In so far as matter and form can be distinguished within it, both are produced simultaneously. In this respect the notion of creation bears a disturbing resemblance to that of emergence. In the case of emergence, however, there is no sufficient reason for the coming into existence of the new entity; its arising is unpredictable and unaccounted for; it is a case of inexplicable and ultimate becoming, and this is what is meant by the term *emergence*. In creation, on the other hand, although there is no material cause, there is an efficient cause—namely, the will of the creator, and that will constitutes a sufficient reason for the coming into existence of the new entity. Such a will must be able to bridge the gap between being and nonbeing; and this consideration leads the scholastics to assert that such a will must be possessed of infinite power, and, consequently, that only the Deity can create. If this be true, it is obvious that creation is something utterly without parallel in human experience.

Is creation, then, an intelligible notion? This is a question which we must ask. But before we try to answer it, we must note that many nonscholastic thinkers would contest the assertion that creation is without any analogy in human experience. We are all familiar with the appearance of new entities *in toto* in the form of reflections— the sun in the water or the figure in the mirror. Thus in Plato's speculations space constitutes the cosmic mirror in which the eternal forms are reflected. Let us go further. What of the images of dream, memory, fantasy, or hallucination? Rightly or wrongly the man in the street sees in the mind of the subject the cause productive of these. And what of the private sensa of the epistemological dualist? Many epistemological dualists shrink from employing the term *creation* in accounting for the origination of such entities, and choose to speak of emergence, but with doubtful propriety, for, if it be granted that these entities are genuinely new products, the mind of the subject—or, if one prefer, the organism—seems clearly to function as the efficient cause. Dr. Ewing has courageously decided to employ the term *creation* in this connection.[3] And, by so doing, he has raised an important issue. For, if the subject bring into being its own private images, creation is of everyday occurrence.

This is indeed an amazing situation. So easily, so effortlessly, all of us habitually do what the scholastics assert that only the Deity can accomplish. Our very finite powers suffice to bridge the gap between being and nonbeing. What is even more remarkable: while in memory

[3] *Idealism*, pp. 380-382.

and fantasy the will is active, in dream and hallucination images arise without the conjunction, and even in despite of the conscious will. Moreover, the entities which we so easily produce remain private; no volition of ours can alter their status as "wild" data, nor bring about interaction between them and the physical objects of the inferred common world which subsist in public space.

If we are to reject creation, then, must we succeed in establishing some tenable distinction between creation and imaging? It was doubtless a realization of the difficulties involved therein that led Alexander to develop his theory of the squinting mind which would eliminate images altogether, yet the acceptance of his view in the face of Professor Lovejoy's criticism is an alternative so desperate that probably few of us would be prepared to embrace it. Or shall we adopt the other alternative and boldly assert, with Berkeley, that creation is only a divine imaging? In either case difficulties remain. How can a mere volitional fiat produce anything *in toto* and plant it in the external world? It is often said that creation must forever remain unintelligible to us inasmuch as we view it from the point of view of the creatures and not from that of the Creator. It may be so. But that to which I now wish to call attention is the satisfaction which such an admission must bring to the defender of the intermediate position. Either way he wins. If creation be rejected as an unintelligible notion, the dualism between the subsistent world of universals and the existent world of particulars remains, and in the latter brute fact remains unvanquished. If, on the other hand, creation be admitted, it continues to be an unintelligible notion, and the universe remains opaque to reason, for the entire realm of creation constitutes a vast brute fact.

It does not, then, avail the rationalist to invoke the notion of creation. Moreover, by so doing, he concedes that the universe is not rational in itself, that it is rational only when viewed in relation to the will and the purpose of its creator. May it not be the case, however, that the universe is rational *in se,* that its structure is not imposed upon it from without but immanent within it, and may not every particular be so included within that all-embracing structure that it is as essential to the universe as the universe is to it? May not the universe be such a closely co-ordinated whole that a difference anywhere would involve a difference everywhere, that it could not be in any respect other than it is and yet remain the same universe? These suggestions have a familiar ring. Such a universe would be the universe of the absolute idealist, all the parts of which are subtended by internal relations. There is something in these suggestions which makes a perennial appeal, but, we may well ask, does not a sympathetic response to them conduce to wishful thinking rather than to sound reasoning; though it yield emotional satisfaction, does it not subvert the understanding? In the face of vicissitude and pain and moral evil how can such a theory be advanced with any expectation of winning acceptance?

These are queries which the critic does well to raise, and to which we must return in due course. At the moment, however, let us consider certain preliminary questions which, if answered in the affirmative, will quash the absolute idealist's case as soon as it comes into court. Is not the theory before us habitually connected with the two closely affiliated theories of degrees of reality and degrees of truth, and is not the first of these incomprehensible and the second self-contradictory? Moreover, even if it be granted that the universe possesses a rational structure, is it conceivable that any finite mind should discern the outlines thereof? Is it not, in other words, a purely abstract possibility which it is futile to discuss because, although it *may* be true, there is not the slightest reason to think that it is true?

Let us take these questions in their order. With regard to the doctrine of degrees of reality, the principal difficulty—as our hypothetical critic has suggested—is to arrive at any intelligible interpretation of it. If, by *degrees*, he meant the presence of more and less in the sense in which we say, "This is hotter than that," it seems evident that to talk of degrees of reality is to utter words without meaning. A greater degree of intensity is not more real than a lesser; it is only more intense. Again, if it be urged that the more inclusive is the more real and the included the less real, we may once more reply that the assertion is meaningless. Is an elephant more real than an ant? Or is the solar system, which includes both, more real than either? When two entities are both indubitably presented to us, whatever be their relative extension or complexity of organization, must they not both be pronounced equally real? Is not reality, like straightness, a concept which does not admit of degrees? Suppose it to be asserted, however, that one entity is more important and significant than another in the sense that its characteristics are more revelatory of the nature of the whole in which both are included. Whether true or false such a statement is, at least, intelligible; but why call the former entity more real than the latter? To do so is merely to produce confusion. Or will it be said that the real is the changeless? Then the changing will, by definition, be unreal; but what is unreal possesses no degree of reality at all. Or, lastly, will it be urged that one appearance can be more real than another? But an appearance must be a real appearance, or it would not mislead us. When we say that it is an appearance, we mean that it is not what we should naturally at first glance take it to be, and that some of the inferences which we thus draw are erroneous. Thus a man may appear to us in a mirror, and, if we do not realize that we are looking at a mirror, we shall think that he stands where he does not stand. Now the inferences which we draw from one appearance may be more erroneous than those which we draw from another, yet to say that the second appearance is more real than the first is an unfortunate way of speaking which is productive of confusion. Neither is real in the sense that it is what we take it to be, yet each is a real appearance or it would not delude us. Our conclusion, then, must be that there are no degrees of reality.

With respect to the doctrine of degrees of truth the situation is somewhat different, for here we begin with what at least appears to be a clear-cut definition. Truth is taken to be the system composed of all propositions which directly or indirectly imply each other. By definition, then, no proposition is absolutely true inasmuch as it is not identical with the system. Yet, if it be a member of the system, it thereby possesses some degree of truth. We are further told, however, that it is also, in some degree, false. If all that is meant by this statement be that it is not identical with the system, it is at least a misleading mode of expression. Yet more than this seems to be meant, for we are told that, envisaged from the point of view of the Absolute Mind, which alone can grasp as a unified whole the entire system of mutually implicatory propositions, each individual proposition will appear in a different light and as possessing a fuller meaning. It goes without saying that no finite mind can attain to this all-embracing outlook. And this is the important consideration for us, since it may be taken as giving some color to the contention that the universe may constitute a rationally ordered whole even though no finite mind can envisage it as such.

Impressive as this theory may be in view of the number of eminent thinkers who have defended it and the ingenuity which they have manifested in doing so, how can we avoid the conclusion that it is obviously self-refuting? For, since no finite mind can include in its purview the entire system, no finite mind can arrive at absolute truth, and *any* theory advanced by any finite intelligence will be at once partially true and partially false.[4] Now the coherence theory of truth is such a theory; it will, therefore, be only partially true and also partially false. Need more be said? Even if it be partially true, since we, as finite beings, cannot estimate the degree of truth, or yet the degree of falsehood, which it contains, it is surely useless for us. If it be urged that the theory is better than any other, the obvious reply is that we are certainly in a very bad situation indeed. But it would surely be premature to conclude that our position is actually so desperate.

If I thought that the theory that the universe is a rationally ordered system was inextricably linked with the doctrines of degrees of reality and degrees of truth, I, for one, would not consider that it merited further discussion. But, as we shall later see, it is not in fact so linked, and has been actually dissociated from this undesirable con-

---

[4] It cannot, according to this theory, be *absolutely* false if it possess any meaning whatever.

nection. What I wish to do now, however, is to emphasize a consideration which the foregoing discussion has rendered relevant. We have hitherto been proceeding on the assumption that there are three, and only three, possible and clear-cut positions. One is that the universe is fundamentally irrational, and that its rational aspects are only superficial—that such rationality is, indeed, rather apparent than real. The second view is that the universe is partly rational and partly irrational. And the third view is that the universe is wholly rational, and that the human mind may discover the outlines, to some extent at least, of that rational structure.

We now see that our assumption was too naïf. There is, indeed, an intermediate position between the second and the third. It may be contended that the universe is, and must be, rational, yet that its rational structure cannot be apprehended by us, that we cannot see *how* it is rational. Our original threefold division possessed a definiteness which was both convenient and beguiling, but in the course of our discussion the recognition of this fourth possibility has naturally developed, and the consideration of the coherence theory of truth has brought it forcibly before us.

It may be urged that it is difficult to have patience with such a view, that it claims too much or that it claims too little. If the universe be rational, let him who asserts it to be so show that it *is* so; if he cannot show that it is so, let him cease to make the claim. It is difficult not to sympathize with this challenge. Again, it may be contended that, so long as the universe be irrational *quoad nos*, it is futile to speculate as to whether it be rational *in se*. To be impenetrable to human reason, the only kind of reason that we know, is to be irrational. How it may appear to the Deity or to an archangel we neither know nor care. And with these protests, once more, it is hard not to concur.

Nevertheless, the position in question has been defended by a number of thinkers, and not always as a corollary of the coherence theory of truth. Take, for instance, the position of Lloyd Morgan. Beginning with a conception of emergent evolution not very far removed from that of Alexander, he ends by positing beyond that process, as its ground, an eternal Deity. And he does this, not because he believes that the existence of such a God can be directly proved, but because he considers that thus, and only thus, can the universe be viewed as rational. The legitimacy of the assumption consists in its capacity so to rationalize the cosmos. Is this an act of faith? Of faith in reason, or of rational faith, its defender would doubtless answer.

Consider, again, the position of the Reverend John Haynes Holmes in his Ingersoll Lecture on immortality. The argument there is directed to showing that immortality must be recognized to be a fact once the rationality of the universe is conceded, but no attempt is made to prove that the universe *is* rational. We are confronted with a "take it or leave it," with the evident expectation that most of us will take it.

A more eminent example of this way of thinking than either of the foregoing may now be appealed to. How does Bradley proceed in his *Appearance and Reality?* As we all know, he begins by subjecting to detailed criticism every concept in terms of which a philosopher might attempt to conceive of ultimate reality, and by trying to show that every one of them is infected with self-contradic-

tion. What is the conclusion which Bradley then draws?
That the skeptic is right?   Far from it!   His conclusion
is that the human mind, because of the incurably relational
character of thought, is unable to think the absolute as it
is in itself, but that in the absolute all contradictions are
somehow eliminated, and that reality constitutes a self-
consistent, although incomprehensible, whole.

What, once more, is the attitude of St. Thomas
Aquinas?   St. Thomas concedes to human reason at least
as much as does Bradley, since he maintains that it can
demonstrate by its own unaided powers the existence of a
transcendent God and the immortality of the soul.   It
cannot, however, demonstrate that the world had a beginning, although it can see that this is a genuine possibility.
And it cannot grasp the divine essence as it is in itself, nor
can it prove the doctrines of the Trinity or the Incarnation.   Yet, maintains Aquinas, God is, in himself, the supreme intelligible, and the doctrines in question are
thoroughly intelligible in themselves and would be perceived to be so by a sufficiently exalted intelligence.[5]

In this connection we may recall that Meyerson has
insisted with great emphasis, and with equally great plausi-

----

[5] As to the neosupernaturalists whom we considered in the previous
chapter, it is perhaps doubtful how they should be classified with strict
accuracy.   It was convenient to treat of them in connection with the
naturalists and logical positivists whose contempt for pure reason they
share.   In the case of those who reject it, however, their rejection and
their insistence that God is wholly other clearly imply that between the
divine intellect and the human there is no more in common, as Spinoza
put it, than there is between the constellation called the Dog and the dog
that barks.   Whatever, therefore, be the structure of the universe, it seems
clear that it will be unintelligible, not only to the human intellect, but to
any faculty that resembles it.   Accordingly, despite their rejection of the
contentions of emergent evolutionary naturalism, it appears that we are
justified in ranking them with the naturalists as irrationalists.   Those
among them who honestly accept the *analogia entis* should obviously be
associated with Aquinas.

bility, that the conviction that the universe is rational is fundamental to science, and that, although it is a contention which science can never make good—inasmuch as the solution of every problem leaves science confronted by some further irrational—yet it is a conviction which cannot be renounced without destroying the very nerve of the entire enterprise. It may, indeed, be objected that this is just what we ought to anticipate in view of the very nature of science, that science does not raise ultimate problems, and that we have therefore no right to expect that it will yield us an ultimate explanation. But philosophy does raise ultimate problems; consequently we are entitled to demand an ultimate explanation, and to refuse to be put off with appeals to faith, to irresistible conviction, or the like.

The defender of what we provisionally called the "intermediate position," namely, the view that the universe is in part rational and in part irrational, will certainly press this contention for all it is worth against the upholder of the subordinate intermediate position between his own and that of the more extreme rationalist who affirms that the universe is rational but claims to show that it is so. An affirmation not made good and nonproven is, he will exclaim, worthless in philosophy. If we cannot see *how* and *why* the universe is rational, it is a waste of breath to assert that it is so. We no doubt wish that it were, but wishes are not reasons; they reveal a great deal with regard to the psychology of the wisher, but nothing as to the nature of the universe beyond the fact that it includes the wisher. It is both more modest and more manly, and in every respect more becoming, he will contend, to refuse to permit our desires to constrain our thinking, and to follow the argument whithersoever it may lead. It leads, he will insist, straight to his own position, to the recognition that the universe is in part intelligible and in part unintelligible, and there it stops. There, he affirms, we should stop too. To go beyond this point is to pass from terra firma to the realm of airy phantasy where one looks for the pot of gold at the rainbow's end.

We may, for the moment, be content to leave the matter here, and to postpone further consideration of this topic till we come to examine the position of the rationalist, and to inquire how he would reply to these affirmations. With our own basic interest in mind let us now turn our attention to the relation between the position before us and the religious outlook. And first let us ask, if the universe be actually in part rational and in part irrational, which of these two domains is that of religion? Where is its source, whence does it derive its power, and whither does it attract us? To these questions some would certainly reply that religion is rooted in the irrational. The realm of the rational, they would affirm, is the field of knowledge, and the field also of probable hypothesis; to religion belong the shadows and the night, the world of darkness and mystery into which the light of intellect has not penetrated.

Nor would such persons fail to draw some support from sources which would generally be regarded as fully empowered to speak as representatives of the religious mentality, and this at every level of culture. The mind of the savage and the primitive, as everyone knows, is profoundly attracted by the unknown and the mysterious. Fascination as well as fear, even the vital stimulus of hope, impel it in this direction. And, at the highest level, do not the same impulses manifest themselves, and with impressive power? Do not the mystics, many of them at least, put on one side with contempt whatever can be understood as unworthy of the divine? Do they not press on into that "cloud of unknowing" where alone man can encounter Deity? Is not this obviously the motivation that urges men along that *via negativa* which plays so fundamental a part in the theologies both of the East and of the West?

That there is much truth in this contention we must frankly concede, for the facts stare us in the face, and permit of no denial. Yet we may still ask whether this is the unanimous testimony of all religious men, whether history records no opposing voice. Is the adoration of the mysterious and incomprehensible the most exalted emotion which the religious man can feel? When we behold a savage groveling before the unknown we may legitimately inquire whether this is the attitude in which we could most becomingly approach a Deity to whom one applies the term *Father*, and to the theologian expounding his negative theology we may appropriately address the same question. The unknown may well be the terrible, and the fear which it inspires too readily leads to the conclusion that it is so. Here is the source of so much that revolts us in the long history of religion, the hideous practices of human sacrifice and self-mutilation. And when practice gives way to theory, and the rarefied doctrine of a substitutionary blood atonement confronts us, the motive is still the same. When love and trust have arisen, it is because it is believed that something is known with respect to the nature of Deity, that some aspect of the divine nature has been discerned which responds to human aspiration, a goodness which co-operates with human goodness, a compassion which welcomes human devotion.

The theistic hypothesis, as we have seen, is rooted in the conviction that man and God have something in common. It is assumed that it is because he is a rational being that man resembles God, and that it is in the light of reason that the universe is to be interpreted. This is, indeed, a gigantic assumption, magnificient in its metaphysical daring; yet no sooner has it been made than the voice of primitive fear makes itself heard, and assures us that the divine intelligence is wholly other than the human, incomprehensible and inscrutable. It is plain that there is a fundamental conflict here, and one which manifests itself in most of the great religions in affirmation and counter-affirmation. To determine which side we shall favor we must ask ourselves whether man the thinker or man the ignoramus is more worthy of human respect and divine regard, whether trust or fear is the higher emotion, whether it is nobler to seek to understand or to bow in abject awe. If we incline to the former alternative, then we shall hold that religion belongs to the realm of the rational.

Were we, however, to make the opposite choice, and to assign to religion the realm of the irrational, it is none the less evident that we cannot admit that the sphere of the rational is exclusively the property of science. For it is not science, but philosophy, which raises the ultimate questions; to philosophy, therefore, the ownership of this field must be conceded. Consequently between philosophy and religion a radical opposition will obtain, with the result that, so far as religion is concerned, we shall be compelled to ally ourselves with the thoroughgoing supernaturalists.

If we decide, however, to choose the other alternative, how do matters stand? Religion and philosophy will both assert their rights to the same territory—namely, to the realm of reason. What support, then, will religion receive from philosophy?

In response to this question the defender of the position which we are now examining may claim with some plausibility that his theory is capable of rendering to religion a service which no other theory can perform so well. For what is the most crucial of the problems which confront the religious thinker? Beyond all question it is the opposition between good and evil. If the universe be completely rational, how is the presence of evil within it to be explained? If it be basically irrational, how is the status of the good to be vindicated? But, if the universe be in part rational and in part irrational, the answer seems obvious. The good will pertain to the sphere of the rational, and evil to that of the irrational.

From a metaphysical point of view the opposition between good and evil will remain insoluble, since that opposition springs from the nature of ultimate reality. But from the point of view of religion, it may be contended, the problem is very well solved. For what is the problem as religion sees it? It is the problem of justifying the ascription of the origin of evil to a good God. To a thinker who is willing to compromise the goodness of God, the problem, indeed, ceases to be formidable; and some there have been who were prepared to do this. In the forty-fifth chapter of Isaiah, for instance, we find the following sentences put into the mouth of God: "I am Jehovah, and there is none else. I form the light, and create darkness; I make peace, and create evil; I am Jehovah that doeth all these things."[6] To the man who wrote these

[6] Isa., 45:66-7.

lines power was the primary and goodness only a secondary consideration. Likewise the modern theologian who
asserts that the divine goodness is different in kind from
human goodness, and that consequently divine acts must
not be judged by human standards, is at bottom of the
same opinion.[7] Some there are, however, who will welcome Plato's passionate asseveration that to compromise
the divine goodness is the worst form of atheism, and,
consequently, that God must be regarded as the cause only
of good effects. And to the view which we are considering
this attitude is congenial.

The doctrine of a finite God has been frequently
brought forward during the last century, and, despite the
distaste which it arouses in the orthodox mind, demands
respectful consideration, if for no other reason, because of
the moral and religious earnestness of those who have advanced it. According to this theory God is surrounded by
an environment which he did not create, which he finds to
some extent, but only to some extent, malleable, and upon
which he is ceaselessly endeavoring to impose his will. He
is, so to speak, in the position of a powerful administrator
who is perpetually at work trying to establish law and
order, to eliminate iniquity, to redress injustice, to remove

---

[7] It is true that the theologian also asserts that evil always issues in the
production of a greater good, yet he further asserts that God is omnipotent,
and it is clear that a Deity who was, in the literal sense of the word,
omnipotent could produce good effects without antecedent lesser evils.
One must, of course, acknowledge that, in so far as he follows St. Thomas,
the theologian will not ascribe to God omnipotence in such a literal sense.
He will concede that the Deity cannot violate the laws of logic. And
could all evil, as unfortunately it cannot, be shown to result from such a
limitation, one of the greatest obstacles to the acceptance of the theistic
hypothesis as a satisfactory explanation of the universe would be removed.
Yet it would still be the case that God was limited by a reality external
to himself, although, interestingly enough, it would be by the rational,
and not the irrational, nature of the universe.

abuses, and to relieve the oppressed, to vindicate the right. Engaged in this stupendous task he summons man to become his co-worker, and to co-operate with him in the realization of a common and righteous purpose. This is a summons which may well call forth an enthusiastic response. The character of such a God is one to awaken unbounded admiration and heartfelt gratitude. Upon any particular occasion his power to help us may prove insufficient, but of his will to do so there can be no question. He is emphatically one to inspire confidence and to arouse loyalty. And it is possible that our efforts may actually prove useful to him, that, if he help us, we may also help him, as the most obscure private may contribute something to the carrying out of the plans of the commander-in-chief.

The upholder of this view may contend with some plausibility that his position is that of a *pure* theism unadulterated by any influence proceeding from an alien source. The attempt to identify a personal God with the Absolute One results, he may urge, from the confusion of two originally distinct currents of thought. In the first place there is the pantheistic impetus which exalts *mind* at the expense of *minds*, which regards personality as an ephemeral appearance and sees in its dissolution the necessary preliminary to spiritual deliverance, and which envisages ultimate reality as a sea of impersonal consciousness. That the tremendous emphasis upon unity which inspires singularistic speculations of this type corresponds to some deep need of the human spirit we may readily admit.[8] Yet the believer in a finite God will point out that in its depreciation of the significance of personality it

<hr>

[3] To this subject we shall return in the ensuing chapter.

stands at the opposite pole from theism. Theism, he may well claim, is the legitimate philosophical successor of primitive animism, each being inspired by a conviction of the high metaphysical status of the self. While it is, of course, a desire for unity which motivates the development of monotheism—as we see in Plato's conclusion that there must be a "best soul"—yet the unity thus sought is of another type than that which satisfies the pantheist—a unity, not of stuff, but of purpose. And it is the unifying of this stream of thought with the current of pantheism which has produced the enigmatical Deity of orthodoxy.

In all this we must, I think, concede that there is much which merits a sympathetic evaluation on the part of a religious thinker. None the less, when we contemplate the doctrine of a finite God as it stands, we can scarcely fail to see that it is confronted by very serious difficulties. In the first place it is evident that the two objections which we advanced in criticizing the notion of an ultimate opposition between a morally good and a morally evil intelligence apply here also. For, whatever be the nature of the environment external to a finite God—be it lifeless matter, a congeries of relatively unintelligent psychoids, or what not—any hope that God will at last succeed in completely subjugating it would seem to be clearly fatuous. If God's struggle to dominate his environment has always been going on, surely it will go on forever. We must, then, renounce that buoyant optimism so characteristic of religion. This is not, indeed, a logical objection, yet it is one to make us hesitate; for an optimism so universal and impressive may well be based upon solid grounds, even if only obscurely apprehended. And, in the second place, there is the consideration that the facts before us, so far as we are justified in drawing any inference from them at all, suggest that the forces of evil are gradually losing out, that good is inherently stronger than evil, a conclusion that appears incompatible with the notion of a finite God. If it be said that the occurrence of any struggle at all is incompatible in the notion of a good and omnipotent God, we may reply that this suggestion, so far as it is apropos, serves only to engender doubt as to the soundness of the theistic hypothesis in *any* form. And if it be urged that the idea of a *growing* God will account for such progress as the facts reveal, we may recall that we have already examined the notion of ontological growth and found it untenable.

There are, moreover, two further pertinent objections to the doctrine of a finite God. It has been claimed that the doctrine removes the difficulty presented to religion by the reality of evil. But does it, in fact, do so? A finite God will certainly possess much greater power than man, otherwise he would not be called God. Yet is it not plausible to suggest that much of the evil which is actually present in the world might very well be removed by a power only very moderately superior to that of man? One is reminded in this connection of the statement, so diverting in its naïveté, in the first chapter of the book of Judges: "And Jehovah was with Judah; and he drove out the inhabitants of the hill-country; for he could not drive out the inhabitants of the valley, because they had chariots of iron."[9] As Hume and McTaggart have both pointed out, once it be acknowledged that the power of God is finite, there is no way of determining a priori precisely how powerful God is. May we not in the end thus be left with

[9] Judg. 1:19.

the conception of a God who is completely good yet completely impotent?

Lastly, if the finitude of God be conceded, how can we be sure that he is the only God? Why may there not be a plurality of gods? Polytheism has generally been esteemed an incredible hypothesis because it was believed that it could be shown that God is both infinite and creative. Yet we have seen how difficult it is to render the notion of creation intelligible. Again, if we waive this point, how can we be assured that one finite God may not have created one part of the universe, and another finite God another part? Why may not a plurality of deities cooperate in the realization of a common design? And, if the notion of creation be rejected, how is monotheism to be established? Even if the argument from design convince us that the portion of the universe which we inhabit is under the control of a single deity, how can we determine the extent of his power, or what condition prevails beyond the limits of his jurisdiction? These suggestions no doubt seem wild, yet only because they are unfamiliar. Once the infinitude of God be called in question, they inevitably arise and must be reckoned with.

It may be contended, however, that we have succeeded in making the idea of a finite God appear ridiculous only because we have handled it, as it were, *in vacuo,* as though the Deity were environed by a region of sheer anarchy and darkness, the abode of "chaos and ancient night." Yet matters need not be represented so. I think that there is some force in this objection. Let us, accordingly, revert to the problem of relating the changeless realm of universals to the changing realm of particulars. And let us recall how Plato envisaged the situation.

The universe of Plato is a three-story universe. The topmost level is the locus of interconnected and unchanging Forms. The intermediate stage is the realm of souls —of the souls of men, heroes, daemons, gods, and the "best soul," the supreme God; and since souls do not simply arise and pass away, but persist, it is also the realm of permanence and change. The lowest story is the region of becoming and succession, apprehended in sense-perception. It is a world of show, produced, it would seem, by the reflection of the Forms into space wherein their images are multiplied, thus giving rise to particulars. Both the Forms and space are independent of God, yet he is capable of acting upon the world of becoming, apparently by controlling the process of reflection. Furthermore, according to the *Timaeus*, there is a motion native to space which is only partially amenable to divine constraint.[10]

Although the Forms, souls, and space are all seemingly ultimate constituents of the universe, yet it is clear that souls occupy an awkward position. They may be attracted downward toward the realm of becoming and sense-experience, or they may rise until they lose themselves in the vision of the Forms; and in the *Phaedrus* it is plainly indicated that they may subsequently fall from thence.

The late Professor Whitehead, who owed so much to Plato, sought to improve the situation by eliminating souls and including consciousness in the sphere of becoming, thus reducing the universe to a two-story affair. If, however, our previous criticism of the notion of absolute becoming be sound, it is evident that the fundamental diffi-

[10] I am, of course, aware that Plato's various descriptions are not wholly consistent, and that it is a question how far he intended them to be taken literally and to what extent they should be accounted myth. But these problems do not now concern us.

culty will not thereby be removed. But what if we dispense with absolute becoming, and retain the forms and the souls, the realm of eternity and the realm of persistence, time and change?

There is a philosophy which does not belong to the Platonic tradition, but which has, nevertheless, elaborated a conception of the universe in which such a result is actually achieved. It is the school of Hindu philosophy which is termed the Nyāya-Vaiśesika. Ultimate reality, according to this philosophy, consists of time, space, atoms, souls, universals, and the supreme God. These are the irreducible constituents of the universe; they neither begin to be nor cease to be. Yet God, although not a creator, is a maker. It is he who brings together souls, atoms, and universals in an ordered cosmic system whereof he is the designer. The cosmos thus established does not endure forever; like a worn-out machine it at last goes to pieces; all composite substances fall apart; atoms and souls separate from one another; *pralaya* ensues—a period when the universe is, so to speak, at rest. Then God once more initiates a process of construction; another cosmos is formed, to flourish and in due course to perish. And so the cyclic process continues, and will continue forever.

All this is very meaningless, it may be said, and very dreary; the inhabitant of such a universe would be a prisoner in a metaphysical treadmill. Yet the Nyāya-Vaiśesikas would not accept this criticism. There is, so they tell us, a continual trickle of liberated souls escaping from the world process, and these souls return no more unto birth and death. In this emphasis upon the possibility of deliverance the Nyāya-Vaiśesika philosophy is responsive to that spirit of optimism which is native to religion. It is an

optimism, however, which is qualified by the gloomy reflection that, since the entire number of souls is infinite and
the number of liberated souls is finite, the vast majority
of souls will always continue in bondage[11] and the succession of worlds will never come to an end. Here we have
another instance of that conflict between trust and fear
which is so prominent in the history of religion.

I have thus briefly sketched the principal features of
the Nyāya-Vaiśeṣika cosmology, not because I propose to
examine in detail the working out of its general position
or to defend its conclusions, but because these features appear to me both interesting and suggestive. The universe
which this philosophy depicts lacks a completely rational
structure, not because of the presence therein of any positively antirational or demonic entity, but because the fundamental constituents of reality are simply given and are
not mutually interrelated in such a manner as to form a
transparently intelligible whole. We can see, of course,
that, if there be particulars, there must also be universals;
for, otherwise, no particular could resemble any other
particular. But why should there be any particulars at
all? Again, if there be atoms, these atoms must be extended in space. But why should the universe possess a
spatial dimension, and why should it contain any atoms?
Why, once more, should there be any souls, and, if there
be souls, why should there be one supreme soul?

In this connection it may be worth while to recall that,
as Meyerson was fond of pointing out, materialism itself
was animated to some degree by a rationalistic impulse.
It was the materialist's contention that, given his moving

[11] Thus Hindu philosophy provides a correlate to the Christian-Jewish-
Moslem doctrine of eternal damnation.

atoms and the space wherein they moved, he could account for all phenomena in the terms of the motion of particles and their aggregation and dissociation. Yet the particles themselves, their motion, and the space and time in which they moved could not be accounted for, but must simply be taken as ultimate. And what was even worse, secondary qualities and psychical occurrences could neither be accounted for nor even recognized, but only ignored. The naturalist has sought to remedy these deficiencies by his doctrines of absolute becoming and emergence which we have seen reason to reject as untenable. Now the Nyāya-Vaiśesika philosophy would seem, at first glance at least, to be in a better position than either materialism or naturalism, inasmuch as, before beginning operations, it has provided itself with a greater variety of ultimates which has been carefully thought out so as to account for occurrences of every type, so that there is no need to close one's eyes to any aspect of the universe or to introduce at any subsequent stage unintelligible notions such as that of absolute becoming. Hence, when we contemplate it, we experience a certain feeling of relief such as the ancients must have felt when they turned from the flux of Heraclitus to the philosophy of Empedocles with his four roots plus love and strife, to that of Anaxagoras with his mixture and his νοῦς, or to that of Plato with his Forms, his space, and his Demiurge. To the man in the street, at least, the recognition of the union of permanence and change seems to bestow intelligibility upon both; hence the perennial attraction of Aristotle's philosophy with its interacting substances, its form and matter, its four causes, its unmoved mover, and its potentially infinitely divisible space and time.

It is, of course, a question whether this relief be not delusive, whether the notion of a changing permanent will not prove under examination to be as untenable as that of absolute becoming. Thus many idealists have argued. But this is a question which we may postpone until we come to consider in detail the rationalist's position. There is, however, another consideration which the Nyāya-Vaiśeṣika philosophy forces upon us. The ultimates which that philosophy posits do, indeed, constitute a system, yet that system exists *de facto* rather than *de jure*, inasmuch as its various constituents do not all appear logically to entail one another. Their existence is established as the result of empirical enquiry, and not by a process of a priori deduction. In this sense the system falls short of the thoroughgoing rationalist's ideal of a completely intelligible structure. Yet it may be doubted whether the rationalist be justified in making such a demand of the ultimate. Is it not one thing to insist that the part must stand in some intelligible relation to the whole, and another to seek to interpret the whole in terms of a category included within it and properly applicable only to the part?

This question opens up a further line of reflection. We have hitherto been using the phrase "a rational universe" as though its meaning were entirely definite and immediately apprehensible, and therefore one in regard to which no misunderstandings could arise. But, after all, what do we mean by a rational universe? May there not be various senses in which the universe may, or may not, be rational? And, if so, may it not be rational in one of these senses, and not in another? May not rationality conceivably admit of degrees? It is important to clarify our minds with respect to these queries, for, if we address to the universe a confused question, we must not be astonished if it return a perplexing answer. Accordingly, it is with the consideration of this topic that we had best begin our examination of the rationalist's position.

CHAPTER III

RATIONALISM

WHAT DO WE mean, let us ask once more, when we speak of "a rational universe?" In what various senses may this phrase significantly be used? In the attempt to reply to this question I shall now enumerate a number of senses in which it may be, and actually has been, understandably employed, without, I trust, any important omissions.

(1) The universe may be termed rational if the so-called "laws of thought," and the laws of logic and mathematics hold true of it. If these laws have only a pragmatic value in so far as they enable us usefully to correlate to some extent the data of experience, or if they are to be ascribed merely a psychological status determinative of the way *in* which we think, although not of the nature of that *of* which we think, the universe will not in this sense be rational; and if they hold true only of a part of the universe, then the universe will be only in part rational.

(2) The universe may be pronounced rational in so far as it is coherent, in so far as it displays no "rough edges," in so far as it is not a mere aggregate but an ordered whole. Thus, even though all the various parts of the universe be each in itself unified and self-contained,

yet, if these parts fail to supplement or complement one another, but rather jar and clash, the universe will not be in this sense rational. If, on the other hand, the universe constitute a structural unity, even if the order manifested do not appear to be necessitated, and if another possible arrangement may equally well be conceived, the universe will be, in this sense, rational.

(3) The universe may be called rational in so far as it is expressive of a rational purpose. This affirmation raises, of course, a further question as to what constitutes a rational purpose. If we term rational any purpose the fulfilment of which involves the adaptation of means to ends and the completion of some structural design, Satan might be said to act as rationally in organizing the administration of hell as God in establishing the Kingdom of Heaven. If, however, we refuse to acknowledge the rationality of any purpose which does not aim at the realization of what is supremely good, the case stands otherwise; no amount of mere ingenuity or cleverness will meet our requirements. In the first instance we mean by reason what has sometimes been called the logical faculty, the capacity for universalizing and for abstraction and practical adaptability; in the latter instance we expand our conception of reason to include the intuitive apprehension of value. The distinction is that between διάνοια and νόησις.

(4) The universe may be accounted rational if it possess an intelligible structure; that is, if its parts be interconnected in such a way as mutually to necessitate one another. This notion of rationality is more inclusive than our first concept, which to some extent it resembles, inasmuch as the metaphysician may recognize as necessary propositions or relations with which the ordinary logician

does not concern himself, such, for instance, as those which form the basis for ethical and aesthetic judgments, as well as others of purely ontological import. Thus Professor Broad has suggested that the idea of causation may be an a priori concept;[1] and McTaggart has advanced as necessary two propositions which play a fundamental part in his system, namely, that no substance can be simple and that no self can include another self. This conception of a rational universe differs from the third in that it regards the intelligible structure of the world as completely inherent within it and in no way imposed upon it.

(5) The universe may be termed rational if an intelligible answer can be returned to the question: Why does the world exist? And such an answer will inevitably consist of two parts. In the first place, it must be shown that the ontological argument is sound, with the result that it will be seen that the existence of God cannot be denied without falling into logical contradiction; and, in the second place, it must be shown that God does not create the world in consequence of free choice, but that it is either contained within his own being or is necessarily produced by him.

Perhaps it would be well to designate these five senses in which the universe has been called rational by appropriate names whereby they may hereafter be conveniently referred to. The first we may well call the *scientific* view, not only because most, if not all, scientists would subscribe to it, but also because, had it not been originally entertained, the whole scientific enterprise would never have got under way. The second we may nominate the *co-*

[1] *Examination of McTaggart's Philosophy* (Cambridge, 1933), I, 45-46.

herence view, bearing in mind that we are to interpret this term in a purely factual, and not in a logical, sense; the world as a whole is observed to exhibit a certain harmony or continuity which justifies us in referring to it as a *universe* rather than a *pluriverse*, but our ground for so doing is purely empirical. The third we may term the *teleological* view, inasmuch as the universe is regarded as expressive of a divine purpose which is directed toward the realization of values. The fourth we may christen the *necessitarian* view, since the structure of the universe is held to involve relations of logical entailment. And the last we may term, in consideration of the argument upon which it depends, the *ontological* view. Let us now examine these various positions in turn.

The scientific view is one which will not detain us long, for, as we have seen, the denial that the universe is rational in this sense would involve us in self-contradiction. To assert that the laws of thought are not the laws of being is implicitly to deny that they are even the laws of thought; otherwise such an assertion would be psychologically impossible. It is, therefore, quite evident that the universe is, in this sense, thoroughly rational.

The coherence view is likewise one which will not long detain us; for it seems clear that, to affirm that the universe is rational in this sense, is to assert either too much or too little. If inquiry reveal to us that the universe, as a matter of fact, possesses a systematic and coherent structure, and yet if there be no principle which constrains it so to do, this structural coherence will be purely accidental. It will constitute, as it were, a *pose* which the universe has assumed, but which it may at any moment throw off. If the coherence which it manifests be other than accidental, if it be involved in its very nature, it must be in some way necessitated. This means, obviously, that it must be rational in one of the remaining senses, the teleological, the necessitarian, or the ontological.

There is, however, a further consideration. Even if in the nonmental world the occurence of the seemingly haphazard can be shown to be explicable in terms of natural laws, the fact remains that upon this planet the evolution of life has been accompanied by a vast amount of waste, of pain, and of moral evil. To attempt to dismiss all this evil as mere appearance, to try to explain it away as a delusion, is a fatuous undertaking; for, as McTaggart has so acutely observed, the delusion that evil exists would be itself an evil.[2] Hence, if the universe be rational at all, it must be rational in a sense which is compatible with the recognition of this noxious fact. The goodness of the whole must be compatible with the evil of the part, the rationality of the whole with the irrationality of the part. To attempt to show that the universe is, or can be, or must be, rational in such a sense may well appear a desperate venture; yet, if there be a possibility of achieving it, it seems clear that this possibility can be realized only by showing that the universe is rational either in the teleological, the necessitarian, or the ontological sense.

The defender of the intermediate position is never tired of stressing the difficulties involved in such an enterprise. And he is, of course, right in so stressing them. Nevertheless, his own position is by no means so free from difficulties as it appears at first sight. It is, indeed, characteristic of theoretical compromises, or doctrines elaborated to

[2] See *Some Dogmas of Religion* (London: Edward Arnold & Co., 1930), pp. 209-210.

defend a middle ground, that they tend, when contrasted with either of the extreme views, to produce an impression of sanity and plausibility. But the question is always whether this impression will be borne out, or, on the contrary, dispelled, by a rigorous scrutiny. And, in the present instance, such scrutiny has proved in the highest degree disillusioning.[3]

The theory that the universe is partly rational and partly irrational requires that the two principles be kept mutually distinct, for if they blend they will no longer constitute two independent principles, and the result will be a collapse into monism. Yet their co-operation has been assumed to be necessary to account for the actual universe, and for this express purpose has their existence been posited. It appears, therefore, that these are expected to perform a task for which their very natures incapacitate them.

Let us suppose, however, that they can co-operate and yet remain distinct, each being uninfected by the other. They will, then, either be in a state of equilibrium or one will gain upon the other. If one gain upon the other, it must be ontologically prior to the other; the latter will, therefore, be subordinate, and its independence is thereby qualified. And, if one have been gaining upon the other throughout beginningless time, the process should long ago have been brought to a completion, and the universe should have become entirely rational or entirely irrational. Let us, accordingly, assume that they are in a state of complete equilibrium. Then neither will gain upon the other; consequently there can be no increase or decrease of ration-

---

[3] Cf. McTaggart's *Studies in Hegelian Cosmology* (Cambridge, 1917), secs. 160-167, from which the criticism in the text has largely been drawn.

ality or irrationality in the universe. Now experience acquaints us with no such static condition. There is not only constant fluctuation but also, through the fluctuations, some clearly discernible moral progress—an extension of order, law, and reason. If the balance be perfect, there must, somewhere or sometime in the universe, occur counterbalancing triumphs of irrationality and evil. This is an astounding hypothesis, one which would have practical consequences of a devastating kind, and, certainly, one which could be seriously entertained only after the presentation of cogent proofs. Do not these considerations, it may be asked, make it evident that the plausibility of the intermediate view is entirely superficial, and that actually it is self-stultifying?

It might be urged, however, that we are going too fast; as we have distinguished various senses in which the term *rational* can be used, so we ought to distinguish corresponding senses of the term *irrational*. We have, indeed, acknowledged that the universe is rational in the scientific sense; and this means that it is, in this sense, rational all through, for the laws of thought apply to any and every sort of reality, and that to which they apply cannot be completely chaotic. Everything, therefore, is rational in this sense. Yet, may it not be the case that part of the universe is rational *only* in this sense, and therefore irrational in the other four senses, while the rest of the universe is rational, not only in this sense, but also in the coherence, the teleological, the necessitarian, or the ontological sense? Again, in connection with these last four senses, ought we not to distinguish between the irrational and the anti-rational, between that which is merely indifferent to the claims of reason and that which is actively opposed to them? May not both factors be present in the universe? It is difficult, indeed, for reasons which we have already noticed, to entertain seriously the hypothesis of a cosmic, preverted will, a Satan coequal with and eternally opposed to a good God. But may there not be some blind yet destructive power which is a permanent constituent of the universe and always active therein?

Some such state of affairs was actually envisaged by Plato when he wrote the *Timaeus*. And the fact that such a mind as Plato's could entertain and elaborate such a world view gives us pause, for who could fail to take seriously an hypothesis advanced by one of the greatest thinkers, if not the greatest, who ever lived? Space, as he conceives of it in the *Timaeus*, is nonrational in character in the sense that it constitutes a brute fact, in that its reality is not implied by, and is underived from that of the Forms or the Demiurge. It is ultimate, as they are ultimate; yet it is in no way opposed to them, it is merely indifferent to them. The motion, however, which is native to space is an obstacle, not with respect to the Forms which remain in eternal aloofness as indifferent to it as it is to them, but to the constructive activity of the Demiurge, to whose efforts to maintain a world system modeled upon the Forms it constitutes a perpetual threat. In this sense it is positively antirational. Thus in the *Timaeus* we have what is probably the most impressive statement of the intermediate point of view to be found in the entire history of philosophy. What are we to say of it?

In the first place, there is this to be said: There is nothing in the nature of the Forms that involves the existence of space, and nothing in the nature of space that involves the existence of the Forms. The relation between them is purely accidental. It is purely accidental that space is capable of acting as the receptacle of the images of the Forms, or that the Forms are capable of being reflected in space. It is upon this purely accidental connection that the existence of the entire spatio-temporal world depends. This is certainly a very amazing state of affairs. Perhaps it will be said that this provides no reason for incredulity. One of the most amazing things about the universe, it might be interjected, is that so many philosophers find it so entirely other than might have been expected. Still, *pace* Tertullian, the fact that an hypothesis impresses us as amazing is not a sufficient reason for accepting it. The feeling of incredulity which is aroused by the suggestion that the existence of the entire world of particulars is the result of some cosmic accident *may* be due to mere prejudice, yet there is no doubt that we should experience much more intellectual satisfaction if in its stead we could elaborate some theory involving logical necessity.

In the second place it is not very clear how the intervention of the Demiurge renders the whole process more plausible. It is he, of course, who is responsible for the architectural design which is embodied in the world structure. But how does he bring about this result? If space can image the Forms, and if the Forms can be reflected in space, what more is required to account for the spatio-temporal world? Plato evidently believes that a controlling and directing intelligence is required to give the world a structure such that it will correspond as closely as possible to its eternal archetype. The Demiurge is, therefore, endowed with the power of determining how the Forms shall be imaged in space. Are we, then, to infer that, were it not for the Demiurge, such imaging would not occur at all? If this inference be correct, the existence of the spatio-temporal world will depend upon the conjunction, not of two, but of three factors—space, the Forms, and the Demiurge. Each of the three will be a self-subsistent reality, the existence of which in no way necessitates that of either of the two others. This is an even more amazing state of affairs than that which we previously contemplated in which the accidental conjunction of only two mutually independent realities was involved. Were the Demiurge to be replaced by a creative God, upon whose volition would depend the existence of space, the Forms, and all particulars, the situation would become relatively simplified, and the universe would be, in the teleological sense, rational. ·

In the third place, and this is the most important consideration, the relation between the Forms and particulars presupposed by the whole scheme appears to be quite unsatisfactory. The realm of Forms is the domain of rationality, the realm of becoming is infected with irrationality, and Plato is quite aware of the disastrous consequence which would follow from a blending of the two. It is a matter of life and death for his theory, as we have seen, that the two realms should be kept distinct. And it is in this very need that we find the root of the insoluble problem which perplexed him from the beginning to the end of his philosophical career—namely, the problem of providing an intelligible account of the way in which particulars participate in the Forms.

If the Forms be brought down into the spatio-temporal world and made actually to characterize particulars, the rational and the irrational will become blended, and the two opposing principles will, as it were, conspire to produce through their joint activity an ordered cosmos. But this strongly suggests, if it does not absolutely imply, that the distinction between them is only relative; that an ultimate reality must be posited of which they are the manifestations. In this unity one principle or the other will clearly be predominant, and our conclusion must surely be that it is the principle of rationality. The irrational, then, will be so only in appearance, and that appearance will be due to our own limited perspective.

To escape this conclusion it is essential, as Plato saw, that the Forms remain aloof. But then they cannot perform their proper function. Why is it needful to posit the existence—or, if you will, the subsistence—of the Forms? Because the relation of similarity becomes unintelligible unless there be characteristics which particulars possess in common. But if the Forms remain aloof they cannot be thus possessed. To say that the particular resembles the Form gets us nowhere, for this implies that the Form and the particular have something in common; we shall, then, be led to posit a third entity, and so a viciously infinite regress will open before us.[4] The effort to keep the Forms aloof thus ends in failure.[5]

What the gigantic intellect of Plato could not accomplish no lesser thinker has achieved. Modern philosophers who believe in the objective reality of universals bring them down to earth, and envisage them as actually characterizing particulars.[6] It would seem, then, that the inter-

---

[4] This is, of course, the argument from the third man, or one of the arguments called by that name.

[5] Although in the *Philebus* Plato omits the antirational principle—i.e., the motion which is found in space—this omission in no way obviates the difficulties which we have just considered.

[6] This is the theory upon which certain neoscholastic thinkers have bestowed the name *empirical realism*. See R. P. Phillips, *Modern Thomistic Philosophy* (London: Burns, Oates & Washbourne, 1948), II, 104.

mediate position cannot be pronounced tenable, and that, accordingly, we must at long last resort to the rationalistic point of view and ask ourselves whether, after all, the universe as a whole may not be rational in a teleological, necessitarian, or ontological sense.

To be rational in the teleological sense it must be the expression of a rational purpose. A thoroughly rational purpose will, of course, be a good purpose; and this, I take it, means without question that it will aim at the realization of value. If the universe be completely explicable in terms of such a purpose, there can be nothing in it which is not somehow involved in this purpose; that is, there can be no reality which is unoriginated and independent of the divine volition, nothing, in other words, which is not created.

Here we encounter an initial difficulty. If everything in the universe be produced by the divine volition, this will be true of universals as well as of particulars. Many thinkers have not shrunk from the assertion that such is the case, and have insisted that the being of universals depends upon the divine consciousness which contemplates them. Nevertheless, it is difficult to see how this position can be sustained. To argue that a universal must be independent of your mind and my mind, on the ground that we are both aware of it, and then to contend that it must, nonetheless, be dependent upon some mind, and therefore upon the divine mind, is obviously to reason in a circle. If universals be not the product of human minds, there seems no reason to regard them as the product of any other mind. If this be granted, it is evident that the realm of universals—the subsistent world, to employ the popular terminology—is not produced by the divine volition, and is not expressive of the divine purpose. It might still be the case that the entire existent world was produced by the divine volition and did constitute an expression of the divine purpose. But it would be only a portion of the universe, and not the whole of it, which could be so described.

It would also be the case, however, that the existent world could be wholly explained in terms of the divine purpose only if it were created; and the notion of creation is generally conceded to be a very mysterious one. I have already advanced the contention that to the term *creation* no intelligible idea corresponds. Take Aristotle's four causes—the efficient, the material, the formal, and the final—and you have a very good account of what is involved in the notion of making, a notion which experience has rendered thoroughly familiar. Drop out the material cause, and you have left what theologians call *creation*, but with the material cause has not intelligibility been also eliminated? So many philosophers have been willing not only to accept, but also to utilize, the doctrine in question that one is inclined to hesitate before dismissing it, motivated by the commendable suspicion that perhaps they have seen in it something which one has failed to see one's self. A perusal of the writings of these philosophers does not, however, strengthen this suspicion; they generally agree that it is not, and frequently add that it should not be anticipated that it would be, intelligible to the creature who is, as it were, at the "receiving end" of the relationship involved. It is understandable that one who is prepared by an act of faith to accept a so-called "revelation" which professes to be above reason should accept with it such a doctrine, but I confess that to me it seems clearly to have no place in a rational view of the universe.

There remains the problem of evil. It presses with peculiar force upon the believer in a creative God, since such a God might be supposed to have both the will and the power to protect his creation from its intrusion. It is true that orthodox theologians, when they speak of God as omnipotent, do not in general mean that he is able to violate the laws of logic or mathematics. It may be questioned, however, whether these limitations suffice to account for all the evil in the universe, and whether further limitations must not be envisaged. Something has already been said on this topic in connection with the notion of a finite God, and something more must be said hereafter. For it does not follow, from the fact that it cannot explain everything, that the theistic hypothesis cannot explain anything. Though it may not suffice to bear alone the weight of the entire universe, it may, nevertheless, prove possible to include it within a more comprehensive hypothesis which may suffice to bear that weight. This possibility we shall consider in connection with our inquiry as to whether the universe may not be rational in the necessitarian sense.

The universe will be rational in this sense if it possesses a coherent structure, the fundamental parts of which are so interconnected that the existence of any one involves that of all the others, the relations which subtend them being thus neither arbitrary nor fortuitous but necessary. In the realms of logic and mathematics we are already familiar with structures characterized by logical coherence and necessity; the question now is whether such a structure belongs to the existent.

The hypothesis that the universe is rational in this sense undoubtedly possesses one advantage over the hypothesis that it is basically irrational or only partially rational. On the second hypothesis the universe will be at bottom only a heterogeneous aggregation of mutually independent entities, from which it seems clearly to follow that such aspects of regularity and systematic coherence as it exhibits are the product of chance—an assumption which seriously taxes our powers of belief. On the third hypothesis the universe will be the joint product of two mutually independent and antagonistic principles which none the less amicably co-operate to generate a world system— again an assumption which it is hard to credit. But to affirm that the universe is a coherent whole, and that its structure is logically necessitated, is to state a proposition which seems to be spontaneously asserted by the human mind. Historically, it constitutes the primal assumption of science; and, as we have seen, the efforts of empiricists to substitute for it a different assumption—such as the soundness of the regularity view of causality—logically invalidates the entire enterprise.

If it be, then, not merely legitimate but imperative for the scientist to make this assumption, why, one may ask, is it not open to the philosopher to do the same? Many philosophers would reply that this is, indeed, the only intelligent course to pursue. To make such an assumption is, if you will, an act of faith; yet it does not involve irrational faith but faith in reason.

It may be objected, however, that what is permissible for the scientist is inexcusable in the case of the philosopher. Science, we may be reminded, since it raises no ultimate problems, can return no ultimate answers. The purview of science is limited; and, within that limited purview, any assumption which proves fruitful is justified by its practical utility. The scientist is bound to proceed *as if* the universe were rational because otherwise he could accomplish nothing; he looks for the causes of perplexing phenomena because otherwise he cannot explain them; he assumes that the problem before him is soluble, because otherwise he must abstain from investigating it; and, when his solution raises a further problem, he again assumes that this is soluble also. The philosopher's purview, however, is the entire universe; he is concerned, not to experiment, but to understand; to understand is to develop conclusions from basic certitudes; but, if all depend upon a primal act of faith, there are no basic certitudes, and no conclusions can ever be definitely established; his entire undertaking is, therefore, rendered nugatory.

The philosopher, of course, can still defend himself by pleading that his primal assumption is justified by its very inevitability. The position of the full-fledged skeptic is, of course, one of self-refuting dogmatism; for the skeptic claims to possess knowledge in the very act of affirming that it is unattainable. The only possible attitude, other than his own, our thinker may urge, is that of utter indecision and uncertainty; but this is an attitude which it is impossible to maintain in practice; and, yet, the only escape from it is by an initial act of faith in reason.

I think that we can see that this point of view is not destitute of a certain degree of plausibility. As a refuge of despair many will find it more congenial than the position of the irrationalist or that of the defender of the intermediate view. I have devoted this amount of attention to it inasmuch as I have already referred to it as the subordinate, intermediate view. One may be induced to adopt it by such considerations as led us to dismiss the two other hypotheses as untenable. If by reasoning we cannot show that the universe is, in whole or in part, irrational, are we not driven to conclude that it is, that it constitutes, an ordered system, even if that system be too vast for us to discover its outlines?

Clearly, however, we ought not to stop here unless we be compelled to stop here. And are we so compelled? Is there any ground for the supposition that human reason— the only reason with which we are acquainted—is incapable of grasping ultimate reality? If it distort reality in the act of grasping it, we are indeed in a hopeless situation. But how can we know that it does so unless we can compare the distortion with the original?

One of the most ingenious attempts to establish the incapacity of reason to know the Absolute is that of Bradley, to which I have already referred. Thought, inasmuch as it connects subject with object, is relational; and relation, like every other category, maintains Bradley, involves us in contradiction. If A and B be united by the relation r, r must, he argues, be related to both A and B. This involves two other relations, and these, in turn, must be related, on the one hand to r and A, and on the other to r and B, and so on ad infinitum. This infinite is vicious, since, unless it be completed, A can never be related to B. His conclusion is that relation is only appearance, that ultimate reality is nonrelational, and that thought, being infected with unreality, cannot conceive it as it is.

It is evident that, in so arguing, Bradley treats relations as though they were not relations at all, but entities of another sort, such as substances or qualities. Substances and qualities are connected with each other by relations, but a relation does not require another relation to connect it with its terms; if it did, it would not be a relation.[7] Once we grasp this fact, Bradley's argument collapses.

It is unnecessary, however, to maintain that the very notion of relation is self-contradictory to sustain the contention that human reason cannot attain to the Absolute. The same conclusion follows if we accept the coherence theory of truth together with the associated theory of degrees of reality—two doctrines championed by Bradley himself. For, if no finite mind be capable of comprehending in a single and synoptic intuitive glance the entire cosmic system, including its remotest complexities and ramifications, together with all the particulars which it contains, no finite mind is capable of grasping what, by definition, constitutes reality. What it does apprehend will be only a portion—who knows how extensive a portion?—of the universe, and this not as it actually stands in relation to the whole, but in a limited, and therefore distorted, perspective. According to this theory, then, the universe as a whole is at once rational in itself and unintelligible to us.

We have seen reason, however, to reject both these kindred doctrines. We have no ground, therefore, for concluding that the human mind is not *capax realitatis,* in the sense, at least, of being able to discern in some of its broad outlines the general structure of the cosmos, even though the limitations of our finitude debar us from attempting to deduce the necessity of the existence of the various particulars subsumed under them. This is a modest claim compared with the magnificent pronouncements of Spinoza and Hegel; yet it will, of course, be scouted by

[7] See McTaggart's *Nature of Existence* (Cambridge, 1921), I, sec. 88. Cf. my *Conception of God in the Philosophy of Aquinas* (London: George Allen & Unwin, Ltd., 1933), p. 381.

every empiricist. I am persuaded, nevertheless, that there are convincing arguments which constrain us to regard the universe as constituting a coherent and rationally ordered system. I do not pretend, however, that there are no difficulties in the way of so regarding it. Various philosophers have believed that they have succeeded in removing these difficulties, and, in some instances, they have elaborated very interesting and suggestive theories which may well contain the germ of a satisfactory solution of the problem in question. But, in more than one case, I find myself as dissatisfied with the proposed solutions as I am with the reiterated contention of the pragmatists, phenomenalists, and empiricists that every solution is in principle impossible. These problems, I would urge, constitute rather the field in which more work emphatically needs to be done; they are, in my judgment, among the live issues in philosophy, and I shall, at a later stage of our discussion, touch briefly upon them. But, since I see no grounds for regarding them as, in principle, insoluble, I would also urge that the fact that they have not yet been solved provides no justification for rejecting the positive arguments in support of the view that the universe is rational in the necessitarian sense.

In discussing these arguments, it must be remembered that the necessitarian view is not the ontological. We are not trying to answer the questions: Why does the universe exist? Or, why is reality real? What we are trying to show is that in the actual universe the parts stand in a necessary relation to the whole, so that the whole constitutes a coherent structure in terms of which the parts can be explained. One of the arguments which impress me as so convincing is that which has already been developed by Dr. Ewing in connection with his critique of the regularity view of causality.[8] He has there contended that for various reasons, the most important of which we have already noticed, contiguity and succession do not suffice to constitute the causal connection, and that there must be present also a relation of logical entailment.[9] This is, of course, an internal relation, internal in the last of the ten senses which Dr. Ewing distinguishes; in the sense, that is, that it involves that the nature of each of its terms be logically dependent upon that of the other.[10] It is true that Dr. Ewing does not maintain that we can actually discern the presence of this relation, except in the case of certain occurrences of a psychical nature;[11] but he contends that, in the case of the external world, we are compelled to assume its presence even though we cannot detect it empirically.

It may be objected that this is only another manifestation of the vicious habit of presupposing what we cannot prove but wish to prove and that it ought, therefore, to be sternly discouraged. Nonetheless, reasons may be urged in favor of this hypothesis which are of unusual cogency. In the first place, if we accept the regularity view of causality, we are faced with the occurrence of multitudinous events, and multitudinous series of events, in an unnecessitated regularity of order which is absolutely incredible. In the second place, as Dr. Ewing has pointed out,[12] our knowledge of the physical world—if there be

---

[8] See his *Idealism*, pp. 151-194.

[9] He does not, be it observed, attempt to reduce causality to the relation of logical entailment, for this would be to neglect its temporal aspect. Rather he appears to regard it as a complex relation which has not yet been successfully analyzed, but of which logical entailment is a constituent (*ibid*, pp. 168-169).

[10] *Ibid.*, I, 136, 183.   [11] *Ibid.*, I, 176-180.   [12] *Ibid.*, I, 180.

a physical world—is both indirect and imperfect; hence there is no occasion for astonishment at our inability to discern there the presence of the relation in question. And, in the third place, if we can in some cases apprehend it as actually present in the mental world—if we are, for instance, justified in regarding a man's sorrow in learning of the death of a friend as logically conditioned by his love for that friend, as, I think, we are[13]—the extension of the relation to the physical world can surely be defended as a perfectly legitimate hypothesis.

If this much be granted, the concession is fraught with momentous consequences. For, since every occurrence in our world is causally connected, directly or indirectly, with every other, it follows that the universe with which we are acquainted constitutes a system wherein all particulars are interconnected by relations of logical entailment.[14] This conclusion, the importance of which can hardly be overestimated, acquires, I believe, some additional, though indirect, support from our previous critique of the notion of event. If I be right in my contention that the notion of event is a relative one, that every event presupposes prior realities which are not events, it seems evident that these realities must be substances, i.e., entities which have qualities and stand in relations but cannot be reduced to qualities and relations, which do not exist *in alio* but in their own right. Now, while a succession of ultimate and unnecessitated events certainly could not constitute a rationally ordered and logically necessitated system, there is no

---

[13] *Ibid.*, pp. 176-177. I should myself view this as more than a "faint glimmering" of "a priori insight," which is all that Dr. Ewing modestly claims.

[14] *Ibid.*, p. 181.

reason why a number of substances—however great that number be—could not do so.

The second argument is based upon the connection between rational selves and values. Values, of course, as objective realities, fall in the class of universals. Now the last end, or τέλος, of the self can be defined only in terms of the realization of values. The self which has become what we desire it will be a self in which values have become actualized, and which has caused them to become actualized in its environment. The relation in which the human self[15] stands to values involves, then, not merely appreciation but obligation. The self feels impelled to render them concrete. A self which recognized no values, which acknowledged no moral or aesthetic standards, which felt no impulse, however faint, to strive for its own moral betterment and that of others, to benefit its neighbors, to preserve and multiply beautiful objects, would not be a rational being—it would be the inmate of an asylum. The relation of obligation, therefore, in which the self stands to values is rooted in its very nature. It could not be destroyed and leave that nature unaltered. It is, then, an internal relation. And the counterrelation, in which values stand to selves, is internal also. Values which could not be appreciated and striven for, which were incapable of being actualized, which could not function as the goals of conscious, intelligent beings, would not be values at all. My argument is not that minds produce values, or values minds, but that the nature of either logically entails that of the other, and that both are accordingly included within a single system.

[15] Whether all animals be totally devoid of a "sense of obligation" is a question which we need not now discuss.

Most believers in the objectivity of values will be inclined, I presume, to admit the soundness of this contention. Yet it may be suggested that it does not take us very far, since, if there be values, there are also disvalues, as well as universals which fall in neither class and may well be called neutrals. Let us deal first with the disvalues.

The reality of these I am not disposed to question. Some thinkers, indeed, have sought to explain them away as mere negations. But this course, emotionally attractive as it doubtless is, appears to me hopeless. We must then say, I suppose, that diabolical animosity is mere absence of love, that in a fetid mass of corruption we observe mere absence of beauty, and that what I feel in my finger when I touch a lighted match to it is mere absence of pleasure. I can only report that such does not seem to me to be the case. It is true that the actualization of disvalues is productive of disorder and chaos, even as the actualization of values is productive of order and symmetry; but this does not show that disvalues are not as positive in their way as values are in theirs.

It may be urged, however, that, inasmuch as disvalues neither complement nor supplement values, but stand in radical opposition to them, it is impossible that the two groups should be united in a single system, or that the reality of the one should involve that of the other.[16] The objection, I confess, does not impress me as a fatal one. There are plenty of instances in other fields of opposing entities which fall within a common system; we are familiar with the ideas of positive and negative numbers, and positive and negative charges of electricity, and with the

[16] This consideration has been called to my attention by Professor James Rikard of Roanoke College.

square of opposition in logic. Let us, however, consider disvalues as they stand with respect to the self. Here, once more, we discover an internal relation. If the τέλος of the self consist in the actualization of values, it obviously involves a process of purgation, of the elimination of disvalues both from the self and from its environment. Evil and ugliness, wherever found, must be eradicated or minimized as far as possible. This, again, is a matter of obligation. A self which did not recognize this obligation would acknowledge no moral or aesthetic standards, and would not be a rational self. A disvalue, moreover, is that which ought to be rejected, opposed, and negated. It is true, then, that the self and disvalues cannot be conceived in isolation from each other, that the nature of either entails that of the other. It is evident, therefore, that, notwithstanding—or, rather, because of—the opposition between the subsystems of values and disvalues, these two subsystems, together with the selves whose existence they entail, are combined within one, all-embracing system.

What, now, of those universals which we have termed neutrals, which the rational self feels no obligation either to actualize or to prevent from becoming actualized—such universals, for example, as redness or circularity? Toward these, one may say, the self is purely indifferent. It can be conceived apart from them, and they apart from it, inasmuch as the nature of neither entails that of the other. Do they not plainly, therefore, fall without the system wherein selves, values, and disvalues are included?

It does not follow, however, from the fact that no direct relation of logical entailment subsists between these universals and selves, that such a relation does not obtain between these universals, on the one hand, and values and disvalues on the other. And we can see quite clearly, I submit, that such relations do hold. For neither values nor disvalues can be actualized without the co-operation of these neutrals. Like soldiers of fortune they are ready to serve with whichever party enlists their aid. Thus the presence of beauty in a painting may also involve the presence of redness and circularity. Eliminate color and shape from your painting, and beauty will have departed likewise. Ugliness, again, cannot manifest itself without the conjunction of such characteristics as violently contrasting colors, bizarre and unsymmetrical shapes, cacophonous sounds, and the like. Moreover, the realization of any purpose, moral or immoral, in the external world cannot be achieved without the employment as means of physical entities which these neutrals characterize—the timbers and bricks, for instance, of which a hospital is built, or the weapons with which an assassination is committed. Consequently, although the natures of selves and of the neutral universals do not directly entail each other, they do so indirectly. We have reason, therefore, to conclude that selves and universals taken together constitute a coherent system which is rational in the necessitarian sense.

The illustrations which I have just employed, however, call our attention to an additional fact. Values and disvalues can be realized through the co-operation of the mutual universals only in the realm of particulars. The existence of these particulars is, therefore, implicated in the reality of the values which are actualized by means of them. Universals and particulars, accordingly, are all included within a world system wherein every entity directly or indirectly entails the existence of every other. Dr. Ewing's argument led us to an identical conclusion with respect to the existent universe—the argument now before us brings in the realm of subsistence. The two arguments are, of course, closely connected, inasmuch as they are both based upon the notion of internal relation in the sense of logical entailment. It is important to observe that neither argument presupposes the validity of the ontological argument, which is still to be discussed. I have not tried to prove that the existence of the universe as a whole is logically necessitated. I have not tried to answer the question: Why is there any reality at all? I have only tried to show, and I believe that I have shown, that, in the universe which actually does exist, particulars and universals are included within a web of necessary relations so as to constitute a logically unified system; that the universe is not a fortuitous aggregation of mutually independent entities, but a whole of which every part involves the existence of all the other parts. If this conclusion be sound, the universe is rational in the necessitarian sense.

Let us now turn to the consideration of the ontological argument. Oceans of ink have already been spilled over this topic, and, doubtless, oceans will be spilled over it in the future; to which we might well seek to avoid adding additional drops, had not the argument planted itself, as it were, in our very path. Perhaps the most common procedure is to dismiss it with the repetition of Kant's dictum that existence is not a predicate. It is doubtful, however, whether this be the most satisfactory course to take, for, if existence be not a predicate, it would seem rather odd that it should habitually and with such facility be ascribed to various entities. Some there are who, following the cue proffered by St. Thomas, propose to regard it as an act;

yet, inasmuch as that which acts must, in some sense, already be, it is clear that circularity can then be escaped only by limiting the notion of existence. Existence is, indeed, frequently distinguished from and contrasted with *subsistence* or *being*, but not always upon the same ground. Entities in the spatio-temporal world are sometimes said to exist, whereas entities not included within this world are said to subsist or to be. Suppose, however, that some entities—discarnate intelligences, let us say—are in time but not in space. Suppose, once more, that the scholastics are right in affirming that God is neither in space nor time. By definition, then, God and discarnate intelligences would be nonexistent. Such usage would be inconvenient and likely to produce confusion.

Particulars, again, are sometimes said to exist, in contrast to universals which *subsist* or *are*. This distinction is found to be so useful in practice that it is difficult to avoid it even if one does not deem it theoretically satisfactory. It seems so obvious that it is possible to conceive that any particular entity—a stone, an ant, or a man—might not have been, that the universe could have got on perfectly well without it; whereas it seems absurd to suggest that justice or redness might not have been. Nevertheless, if we accept this distinction, it would seem to require us to envisage reality as a genus whereof subsistence and existence are species, and this is, perhaps, a doubtful blessing.

In any case it appears quite obvious that the ontological argument could have been elaborated only by a man who believed in the objective reality of universals, and such a man we know St. Anselm to have been. It is true that Descartes, to whom we are indebted for its reformulation, commits himself in the *Principles* to conceptualism; nevertheless, when he is engaged in the discussion of simple natures, he is clearly pursuing a realistic train of thought. The ontological argument begins with the definition of God, which means that it is rooted in the realm of subsistence, and what it essays to do is to bridge the gap between subsistence and existence. Were the argument sound, it would show only that the existence of God is logically involved in and necessitated by the subsistence of the divine nature; that is, it would tell us why the existent is, but not why the subsistent is. For St. Anselm, of course, this presupposition is only provisional. For, having shown, as he thinks, that God exists, he will then envisage universals in Neoplatonic fashion as dependent upon the divine consciousness. This conclusion, however, in no way follows from the ontological argument itself with which we are now concerned.

It is quite fair, then, I think, to say that the fundamental issues which the ontological argument presents to us are two, namely: (1) is there such a universal as Deity? and (2), on the assumption that there is such a universal, must it characterize an actual individual?

The first question is closely connected with Descartes's doctrine of simple natures. Universals which cannot be subjected to analysis will certainly be classified by the realist as objective entities. But does it follow that these various simple universals, or "natures," combine to constitute equally objective entities *in rerum natura?* Some philosophers have thought so; yet it appears highly doubtful whether they have judged aright. The issue is of importance, for is it not evident that Deity cannot be a simple universal?[17] When we speak of God as a perfect

[17] I am, of course, aware that, for the scholastics, all these qualities are

being, do we not mean that he possesses all desirable qualities? Take the famous definition of God in the *West-
minster Shorter Catechism*: "God is a spirit, infinite, eternal, and unchangeable, in his being, wisdom, power, holi-
ness, justice, goodness and truth." Here are ten attributes
predicated of the Godhead. Let us assume that they are
all simple. Must we now hold that they so unite as to
constitute a compound universal? If so, then any and
every nine which we may select from among them will
likewise constitute a compound universal, any and every
eight another, any and every seven—need I continue?
The multiplicity of universals thus postulated would not
dismay me, did I see any necessity for postulating them;
but in truth I see none. In the case of any simple universal we can be sure of its objective reality, for, if it were
not real, we could not be aware of it. But when I think
of justice and wisdom it seems clear to me that I am merely thinking simultaneously of the universal justice and the
universal wisdom, and that I am not also thinking of a
third universal, justice–plus–wisdom.

If this reasoning be sound, it follows that we are justified in rejecting the notion of compound universals. It
might be contended, however, that Deity is not a compound but a complex quality.[18] Yet it is doubtful whether
this suggestion will help us. "A degree of power surpass-

---

somehow fused together in the absolute simplicity of the divine essence;
but their contention I should be prepared to dismiss on the ground that it
violates the law of identity.

[18] "A complex quality," writes McTaggart, "is one which does not
consist of an aggregate of other qualities, but one which can be analyzed
and defined by means of other characteristics, whether qualities or relations,
or both. Thus, if we define conceit as the possession of a higher opinion
of oneself than is justified by the facts, conceit would be a complex quality,
since it is capable of analysis, but not of analysis into an aggregate of
qualities" (*The Nature of Existence*, I, 64).

ing the united powers of all other beings" would be a complex quality, yet it is not what we mean by Deity, for the notion of Deity includes also goodness and wisdom. Were we to suggest "the quality of surpassing all other beings in respect of every excellence," it might be objected that superiority is not a quality, but a relation, and that, although it would doubtless be grounded in the nature of its term, that nature could be analyzed into simple qualities. And if we say, "the quality of possessing a superior degree of every excellence," we should doubtless be told that the characterization of a substance by a multiplicity of qualities does not generate in that substance the quality of possessing all of them. Here we touch upon a highly controversial topic, that of relational qualities; and our conclusion, I think, must be that the assertion that Deity is a genuine universal can be justified, if at all, only by a more extensive excursion into ontology than we can presently undertake.

Suppose, however, that there is such a genuine universal as Deity. Can we show that it must characterize some substance? Unless we can show that *every* universal must do so, I do not see how we can show that *this* universal must do so. It may be urged that a universal is that which can characterize particulars, and that, if some entity never *do* characterize any particular, it never *can* characterize any particular, and, therefore, is not a universal. But consider what this means. In the case of every quality which admits of degrees, every degree of this quality will constitute a subuniversal. On the assumption in question, therefore, every degree of every quality must characterize some substance. Take such a quality as pain. Must we assume that every conceivable degree of pain must be experienced by some consciousness? And must we make a like assumption in the case of moral evil? I should be sorry to have to defend such a hypothesis.

Our difficulty arises from confusing inherent capacity with the exercise of that capacity. The hydrogen bomb, we are told, has the inherent capacity of destroying an entire city. Does it follow that, if it never be so employed, if, as we hope, some agency in the universe will obviate that dire necessity, the statement that it does possess this inherent capacity is false? Clearly such a conclusion would be absurd. And the inference that because every universal possesses the inherent capacity to characterize particulars every universal must at some time characterize some particular would be equally unjustified. May not the general structure of the universe require that some universal characterize certain particulars? Surely it may; and I have tried to show that it not only may, but does, and, in the case now before us, could we demonstrate by some other proof than the ontological argument that God exists, we should have shown that there actually exists a being who does possess the nature of Deity. But it does not appear that the ontological argument of itself suffices to make good this contention.

In our brief discussion of this redoubtable argument we have seen that it presupposes definite solutions of some of the most fundamental, far-reaching, and debatable issues in the realm of metaphysics. This is doubtless the explanation of the fact that it has constituted one of the persistent storm centers of philosophic controversy from its original formulation to the present hour. It is important, however, to recognize that while the ontological argument, could it be made good, would establish the existence of God as a logical necessity, yet, as Professor Lovejoy has pointed out,[19] it would still be possible to ask why the universe exists, unless its existence could be shown to be logically involved in the divine nature. So long as creation is viewed as the result of a free, arbitrary, and unnecessitated choice, the universe will remain a brute fact which could just as well have been dispensed with. Such an hypothesis would, of course, be incompatible with our conclusion that creation is not an intelligible notion. But, could the existence of the universal have been shown to be logically involved in the divine nature, and could the existence of the Deity have been shown to be logically necessitated, the situation would be very different. Then an answer could be given to the question: Why does the universe exist? And much of the fascination of the ontological argument has lain in the hope that it could furnish such an answer.

Our examination of the argument has led us to conclude that it does not provide an answer. Accordingly, if our conclusion be sound, the universe is not rational in the ontological sense. This, of course, gives us no ground for questioning our previous conclusion that it is rational in the necessitarian sense. It only shows that we have raised a meaningless question. To ask why a derived and dependent entity exists is entirely legitimate, for its derivation and dependence proclaim that it does not contain the ground of its being within itself; but to ask why the ultimate exists is to treat it as though it were not ultimate, but derived and dependent, and thus to envisage it as it is not. An unintelligible question, because it is unintelligible, admits of no answer.

[19] See *The Great Chain of Being* (Cambridge, Mass.: Harvard University Press), chap. iii.

We revert, then, to our previous conclusion that the universe is rational in the fourth or necessitarian sense— in the sense, that is, that it constitutes a system of inter-connected entities the reality of any one of which logically entails that of all the others. This is the only hypothesis which we have found tenable. It might be objected, how-ever, that, upon this hypothesis, the presence of moral evil and suffering could in no way be accounted for. In a uni-verse thus rationally ordered, it might be contended, evil should be nonexistent. There should be no actualization of disvalue, even in a minimal degree, but only the maxi-mal actualization of value. Such, unfortunately, is no-toriously not the case. Hence, if our general conclusion be sound, the rationality of the whole must somehow involve the presence of moral evil and suffering in the parts. And how is such a thesis to be sustained?

The rationalist who is also a determinist has attempted to sustain it by pointing to instances in human experience in which the presence of evil is seen to be involved in the realization of a greater good. There is the familiar ex-ample of the painting wherein the beauty of the whole may be said not only to be compatible with, but actually to re-quire, the presence of ugliness in a part. The determinist will call attention, again, to certain virtues, such as courage, endurance, and resolution, which can be developed only through struggle, inevitably involving danger and pain, against embattled evil; and he will also point to such virtues as sympathy and compassion which can be called forth only by the observed occurrence of suffering in others. In all this there is, of course, some truth. The difficulty is that evil, if it is to produce these beneficial results, must be introduced, as medicines are introduced into the organism, in such amount as will produce the desired reaction. Too large injections of it will act as poison. Oppression and cruelty, for instance, when they exceed the capacity of the victim to resist, do not nourish, but blight the development of virtue; they do not refine, but brutalize. We do not need to turn to history for illustrations of this truth; the condition of the world at the present day bears emphatic witness to it. The rationalistic determinist will, doubtless, urge that the overpowering impression of waste, futility, and irredeemable tragedy derived from this spectacle is due to the limitations of our knowledge, that to the more extensive vision of a superhuman intelligence it might be evident that the evil which appears to us most destructive is necessary for the realization of a good which is great enough to justify it, and that "the sufferings of this present time are not worthy to be compared with the glory which shall be revealed in us." But, while we may be willing to concede that this is a remote possibility, it is hard to take it seriously.

Logically considered, the determinist's basic contention that all choice is necessitated is undoubtedly a strong one. A man's acts, he maintains, are conditioned by his nature and his environment. If they did not issue from his nature, they would be sporadic and unpredictable, they would have no connection with his character and history. We all assume, he insists, that a man acts as he does because of the character that he has and the circumstances in which he is placed. Nevertheless, plausible as his argument sounds, it is difficult not to suspect that there is something wrong with it somewhere. The indeterminist presses his contention that, if a man's acts be completely determined, he is practically an automaton; and that to pass moral judgments upon his actions would be as ridiculous as to pass moral judgments upon the operations of a machine. This is a weighty contention, for even the determinist passes moral judgments upon the actions of men, whereas he refrains from passing them upon the functionings of machines; and the indeterminist's assertion that such judgments are apropos in the former case and not in the latter because it was possible for the man to act otherwise than he did, whereas it was impossible for the machine so to do, is very convincing. We revere Socrates for being a good man because we believe that he could have been a bad man, and we condemn Nero for being a bad man because we believe that he could have been a good man. Moreover, each of us distinguishes, in his own individual case, between regret and remorse. We all regret that we do not possess the intelligence of Plato, the self-possession of Socrates, the courage, resolution, and nobility of Washington. But we do not blame ourselves for not attaining to what, we feel, lies beyond our native capacities. We do have remorse, however—that is to say, we blame ourselves—for many deeds in our respective pasts simply because we believe that we need not have done them.

The indeterminist does not claim that the self is ever completely unconditioned by its nature and its environment, nor yet that it is not often completely so conditioned; what he does claim is that at times the determination is not complete, and that the self is then capable of unnecessitated choice. If this be true, the individual, in such instances, can initiate a chain of causation which begins with himself; in other words, he functions as an ontological ultimate. But to concede this, it may be said, is inconsistent with your previous contention that causality does involve necessity. This charge, I am inclined to believe, might be satisfactorily answered in the following way. The self, one could point out, may be simultaneously confronted with several possible causal sequences; in each case the initial causal act will necessitate its consequences, yet the self can decide which causal series is to be actualized. The swing of the axe entails the decapitation of the criminal, and the decapitation entails his death. But suppose that the executioner refuse to swing the axe. He will thereby initiate another causal series. If this contention be sound, the self will not be completely determined by its nature; its acts will to some extent determine what its nature is to be. Such a view may well involve, as Dr. Ewing has observed, a connection between substance and attribute in the case of the self which will be hard to grasp, let alone to defend. Yet the notorious difficulty of this perennial problem strongly suggests that the right question has not yet been asked; and the above suggestion may conceivably provide a clue to the framing of this question.

How can it be possible, however, the objector may continue, that, in a universe wherein all the included entities are interconnected by relations involving logical necessity, any self should at any time be not completely determined in all respects? But let it be remembered that I have not contended that *all* relations involve logical necessity, but only that the causal relation involves it. Must we conclude that, because *some* attributes of every self are thus necessitated, *every* attribute of *every* self is likewise necessitated? I do not see that we must. Yet, it may be asked, is not the indeterminist contending that the actualization of moral values logically involves the capacity of free and unnecessitated choice? Yes, I think that he is. And, if this contention involve a contradiction, his case is, of course, hopeless. But it is important to observe that the indeterminist is not asserting that the same act is at once free and necessitated. He is asserting that moral action involves genuine freedom of choice, that, unless a man be able to do *either* wrong or right, he can do *neither* wrong nor right. And I do not see that this does involve a contradiction.

If the indeterminist's contention be sound, how do matters stand? It follows at once, of course, that a vast deal both of moral evil and of suffering can be satisfactorily accounted for. It follows that the universe which includes moral values and genuinely free personalities could not be so constructed as to eliminate the possibility of the occurrence of an indefinite amount of such evils, and that the rationality of the universe is not only consistent with, but actually entails, this possibility.

It would seem, however, that there remains much evil which cannot be so accounted for. The sufferings of the animal world press upon us with peculiar force. If we were to attempt to account for them in terms of free will, we should have to entertain an hypothesis which, to the average Western mind of today, appears utterly fantastic, but which, nevertheless, commended itself both to many of the ancient Greeks and to the majority of Hindu philosophers—the hypothesis, namely, that selves are capable of rising and falling in the scale of being, so that the human soul may ascend to superhuman, or descend to infrahuman, levels—and to join to it the further hypothesis that it is the character of the self which largely determines its destiny.

That these two hypotheses are apt to impress us as farfetched is due, I believe, in great measure to the fact that for centuries the average occidental has taken it for granted that there are only two possible world views—the view that the universe is the creation of a God, and the view that it constitutes a mass of "brute facts." If I have been right, however, in arguing that both these views are untenable, the situation is somewhat changed. And the two hypotheses before us are clearly more congenial to the world view which we are now considering than to any other. For, if the universe be a system of interrelated substances, and, if some of these substances be simple in the sense that they cannot be divided into parts which are capable of existing in isolation from the wholes to which they belong, then all such simple substances will—unless we accept the notions of absolute creation and absolute annihilation—necessarily be indestructible. Now, for reasons which I have already given, it seems clear to me that the self is, in this sense, a simple substance; and that, consequently, it can neither come into existence nor pass out of existence. If this be the case, it is evident that some, if not all, selves—all those, at least, that become embodied —do pass through a plurality of lives.

As for the second hypothesis, it is not necessary that we interpret it with the strictness of the "law of Karma" and suppose that in every case suffering is the consequence of wrong choice on the part of the sufferer, as well as upon that of others. It will not be unreasonable, however, to assume that, in a universe which possesses a coherent structure wherein values and disvalues are integrated, the

actualization of value or disvalue on the part of the self
will profoundly affect its destiny.

I should not be inclined, therefore, to dismiss these two
hypotheses on the ground that they are unfamiliar to the
Western mind. Doubtless they appear bizarre when
viewed in the light of Christian or naturalistic presupposi-
tions, yet, from the vantage point which we have now
reached, they will be seen to constitute highly plausible
conjectures. We must admit, then, I conclude, that all
evil may conceivably be the result of free choice; but one
cannot wholly discount the possibility that the situation
may be further complicated by the presence of other factors
whereof we are ignorant.

I have now touched upon one of the difficulties to
which I previously referred, and have suggested what appears to me to be a possible solution. There remains, however, an even more formidable problem—the spatio-
temporal aspect of the universe. We have already seen
the difficulty which arises, and the disruption of reality
which results, if space be taken as an ultimate entity logically independent of, and only accidentally related to, the
realm of universals. Time, likewise, has constituted a perennial problem for philosophers. And it is doubtful how
much is gained for ultimate intelligibility by treating both
space and time as abstractions from a more fundamental
reality—space-time. The development of our argument,
it might be urged, does not require us to come to grips
with these, the knottiest and most perplexing of metaphysical problems. While there are, doubtless, serious difficulties to be faced whether one affirm or deny the ultimate reality of space and time, all that our argument requires is that we do not treat them as "surds," as entities

at once ultimate and irrational. But such, it is clear, they cannot be. For our argument has shown that the entire range of universals is integrated, together with the particulars which these universals characterize, in one coherent whole. Hence, if extension and duration be genuine universals, they, and all extended and enduring particulars, will be included within the systematic structure of the cosmos. There will be no possibility of their remaining isolated and aloof. If, on the other hand, the reality of space and time be impugned, it will be because the notions of space and time will have been found to be infected with contradiction; in which case they will turn out to be, not real, but mere appearances, and, as such, they will have to be accounted for in terms of the limitations of our perspective. In neither case, therefore, will the rationality of the universe be attainted.

The contention is sound, and we might, as a matter of fact, let the matter rest there. To do so, however—or so an objector might insist—would be a base evasion of a difficulty which stares us in the face. "You must realize," one can imagine him saying, "that a temporal universe cannot be a rational universe. Time is a 'surd'; and, to make good your case, you must explain it by explaining it away."

Now I am quite prepared to admit that a theory which regards the future as unreal, and which envisages reality as terminating in the knife-edge of the present, and as continuously growing as the past becomes ever longer, and, so to speak, pushes the present before it, is incompatible with the view that the universe is rational. But we have seen that to talk of reality as growing is to speak without meaning. If time be real, future events which are not yet present must be just as real as past events which once were present.[20] And, if the universe possess a coherent structure, that structure must include all these events. If so much be granted, the rationality of the universe is no longer called in question. But, having insisted upon this point, I frankly confess that all that has been said about time by any thinker with whom I am acquainted leaves me with a feeling of dissatisfaction.[21] The problem of time is the most difficult of all metaphysical problems, and the last word, certainly, has not yet been said about it.

"This," the objector might continue, "is not enough. For you have plainly indicated, in your brief discussion of the problem of free will *vs.* determinism, that you incline toward the position of the indeterminist. But it is nonsense to talk of freedom of choice, unless there be real time to make a choice in. And, even if time be real, future events, if the future also be real, will be really determined, and, once more, to talk of free will is nonsense."

I might, of course, remind the objector that Kant taught that the self is completely determined *sub specie temporis,* and yet noumenally free—free, that is, as a nontemporal entity. Time is an order in which it arranges the data, not only of sensation but also of introspection, while remaining itself outside that order. I might even urge that future events, if not logically necessitated by

[20] In this connection I might point to the evidence for precognition recently amassed by parapsychologists.

[21] It seems to me that McTaggart's argument for the unreality of time, as stated in *The Nature of Existence,* II, chap. xxxiii, is completely destructive of Lord Russell's theory of time, against which it was directed, and that it has not been satisfactorily refuted. (See my paper on "Dr. Broad's Refutation of McTaggart's Argument for the Unreality of Time," *Philosophical Review,* L, Nov., 1941, 602-610). I do not see, however, how McTaggart's view of time accounts for the experience of passage, of "living through."

antecedent events, are both real and yet undetermined. Or I might concede that Kant is right in regarding the temporal order as necessitated through and through, and yet maintain that if the self, in arranging its data in a temporal order, be not conditioned by any external reality, but be itself solely responsible for that order, it is free. But, although one can talk in this way, it is very difficult to think in this way. Freedom does seem to involve the genuine possibility of performing either one of two—or any of more than two—different acts, and such a possibility certainly involves the reality of time. What the eternal counterpart of an apparent and temporal act of choice might be it is impossible to imagine, and—to say the least —difficult to conceive.

"This is where your idolatrous pursuit of a rational world view has led you," the objector may exclaim. "You have arrived at a hopeless impasse. A retreat is inevitable." Perhaps—but where shall we retreat to? The problems of time and free will would still press upon us with undiminished insistence. Shall we go the whole way, back to the position of the irrationalist? What will this involve? Does the irrationalist, as we called him, actually reject each of the five senses, which we have subsequently distinguished, in which the universe can be called rational? Undoubtedly he rejects all but the first, or scientific, sense. Does he, however, reject this also? If he does not reject it, how can he acquiesce in a world of pure becoming? If he reject it, how can he argue? Obviously he cannot argue, unless he acknowledge the "laws of thought." Human thinking, he is wont to concede, must proceed in accordance with these—even though he add that the same demand must not be presented to the physical world. But, if any man recognize the law of noncontradiction, by that law shall he be judged. Now the notion of absolute becoming, of the self-initiation of that which is not, clearly flouts this law. And, again, the existence of the physical world which the naturalist posits can be established, if at all, only by invoking the principle of causality in a sense other than that of mere contiguity and succession of phenomena; yet to invoke it in any such sense is to deny the regularity view of causality which is the very cornerstone of the naturalistic faith.[22] This lack of consistency deprives naturalism of any value as a place of refuge for thinkers. Consequently, we must pass through naturalism into phenomenalism, and thence, as we have also seen, into solipsism. This does not look like a strategic withdrawal; it looks like a rout.

Rather than turn in so precipitate a flight I, for one, would prefer to seek refuge in what I have termed the subintermediate position. One might urge that we have found cogent arguments which prove that the universe is rational in the necessitarian sense, but that, because of the inability of the human mind to avoid involving itself in antinomies, we cannot adequately envisage it as rational.

[22] Nor is this all. If the naturalist adopt a representationalist theory of sense-perception, to sustain it he must do more than infer that sensa are produced by some reality upon which they depend. He must also show that this reality consists of entities characterized by such primary qualities as extension and shape. But how can he do this? Plainly he can do it only by making the further—and highly disputable—assumption that a cause must resemble its effect. Visual and tactual data possess extension and shape; if the assumption be sound, their causes will be extended and shaped. But visual data are also colored, and tactual data are hard, cold, sweet, etc. If the assumption be sound, these qualities also should characterize the causes of the effects wherein they are found. Yet, *ex hypothese*, the existence of such qualities can never be observed, since the causes themselves can never be observed. Hence the naturalist, who professes to be nothing if not empirical, is loath to posit them. Yet posit them he must, or else abandon his position. (See McTaggart's *Dogmas of Religion*.)

And the inability to avoid the formulation of antinomies one might attribute, not to any inherent viciousness on the part of human reason, but to the sheer magnitude of certain problems which so exceeds our finite capacity as to inhibit us from framing the right questions, and so from finding the right answers. This is a possible, and, perhaps, even a respectable position; but there can be no doubt that it is a very dangerous one. For, by adopting it, we debar ourselves from arriving hereafter at any solution of the problems which we have thereby pronounced insoluble. The history of philosophy strongly suggests that the wisest course is also the most courageous, to advance straight against the problems with the determination that, having grappled with them, like Jacob who grappled with the angel, we will not let them go until they bless us.

There is, at any rate, no ground for pessimism. It may be that the determinist will ultimately succeed in so stating his case as to save the validity of moral judgments, and to remove the persistent incredulity which his theory has hitherto inspired in many. Perhaps such a flood of light will be shed upon the connection between substance and attribute in the case of the self as to vindicate the attitude of the voluntarist. The reality of time may become so thoroughly established as to silence the objections of the most critical, or the notion of eternity be so clarified that it will be seen to preserve in transfigured form all the values discoverable in the temporal process. When one surveys the achievements of human thought in the past, one's confidence in its future is heightened rather than diminished.

In the preceding pages I have tried to state the considerations which favor the adoption of such a view as I have put forward without claiming too much for them or underestimating the difficulties which remain. Doubtless some would accuse me of having overstated the latter. In any case I cannot but hope that the individual estimate of the present state of philosophical inquiry therein offered may contribute to further discussion. I now propose, in the concluding paragraphs, to consider the relation between the rationalistic position and the religious outlook.

In the first place, what of the theistic hypothesis? I have already pointed out that, in a modified form, it may prove susceptible of being reconciled with the necessitarian view. While a noncreative God could not function as the origin of the universe, he might constitute, as it were, the keystone of the universe. As *primus inter pares* he might stand in a relation of unique intimacy to every other self; his purview might conceivably include the entire universe which would thus be open to his immediate inspection, his influence might be everywhere felt, and his moral character might be such as to claim unqualified homage. Clearly there is nothing self-contradictory in such a notion. Are there any arguments which can be urged in its support?

It is difficult to see how a purely a priori argument could be developed which would support such a theory. One turns inevitably to that school of broad empiricism which takes as its point of departure, not sense-experience alone, but ethical, aesthetic, and religious experience as well. Thinkers of this school are accustomed to lay great stress upon two well-known arguments—the argument from design and the argument from religious experience.

The former argument is, of course, based upon observed regularities which manifest the so-called "laws of nature," and upon the upward trend of the evolutionary process. Its familiarity renders it unnecessary, I think, to restate it here.[23] Obviously, this argument is constrained to wrestle with the problem of evil. It may be urged—and quite truthfully, I admit—that evil is chaotic and parasitic in nature, and that goodness is both constructive and, in the long run, possessed of greater efficacy. None the less, when evidences of design are invoked, it seems plain that some of these will point to intelligences indifferent to ethical considerations. Our general position renders it quite feasible to posit the existence of these; and, in like manner, any evidences of ethical purpose may be referred to good intelligences. The problem will be to show that there is a single, supreme, good intelligence— the "best soul," as Plato puts it. The evolutionary process, it may be said, is one; therefore the directing agency must be one. But how do we know that it is not a "co-operative venture?" The utmost that can reasonably be claimed for the argument is some degree of probability; but *what* degree of probability to assign it is a question which might well perplex the wisest.

The situation is somewhat similar in the case of the argument from religious experience. In this field one always appeals to the mystics as the recognized experts. And the notorious difficulty is that while many, probably the majority, of the mystics are assured that their experience brings them into contact with a divine intelligence,[24] other mystics—in particular the Buddhist mystics —report no such contact, but enlarge rather upon the vision of the eternal cosmic order which, in their moments

[23] For an excellent statement of this argument see the late Professor G. Dawes Hicks's *The Philosophical Bases of Theism*, chap. vi.

[24] For our present purpose it does not seem necessary to distinguish in this connection between the theistic and the pantheistic mystics.

of intuitive insight, they apprehend. Now it might be maintained that our position enables us to provide each type of mysticism with its appropriate object, the theist with a personal God with whom he can enter into a personal relationship, and the nontheistic mystic with an all-inclusive Absolute in which he can feel himself at home; and that, consequently, the validity of each type of mysticism can be acknowledged without impugning that of the other. And this consideration is, certainly, a point in its favor.

There remains, however, the further possibility that the object experienced by all mystics is the same, and that their differences are differences of interpretation. ˙ It is highly doubtful, to say the least, whether we possess at present sufficient knowledge to attempt to decide between these two possibilities.[25] But, even were we to decide in favor of the latter, it might still be contended that the theistic interpretation is the more plausible, could it be shown—as, perhaps, it might—that it is more adequate and more satisfying.

As regards the possible objection that, in an unoriginated, self-existent, and sempiternal universe such as is envisaged in the necessitarian perspective there is no room for a single, supreme intelligence, I think that it can be satisfactorily answered by pointing out that the universe to our certain knowledge includes a vast number of persons, that some of these persons at the human level—such as Alexander the Great or Zoroaster—have exerted a

[25] At some period in the future when the mystics of the various religions have come to practice their devotions together, and have arrived at a far greater degree of mutual understanding than they now enjoy, perhaps it may be possible to arrive at some solution of this fascinating and crucial problem.

tremendous influence upon their environments, and that there is nothing self-contradictory in the supposition that the universe may contain a superhuman person possessed of far greater power and of far greater goodness than these. The real problem for the monotheist, as I see it, is to show there is only *one* supreme self. How can we be sure that the vast reaches of the cosmos may not contain a number of such superhuman intelligences?

This is the inevitable consequence, it may be said, of rejecting the doctrine of creation, and substituting for it the notion of a self-existing cosmic structure embracing a plurality of sempiternal selves capable of rising to super-human levels and subsequently falling from thence—unless, indeed, they attain to complete emancipation from the cosmic process—and equally capable of sinking below the human level and subsequently regaining it. But is the situation really so simple? Even if we grant that creation is conceivable, does it inevitably follow that there is only one Creator? How do we know that the world process may not be a joint enterprise initiated by a group of creators? Or how do we know that each creator may not create a world of his own? The mediaeval thinkers were sure that there was only one Creator because they were satisfied that multiplicity in any form was always the result of ante-cedent composition, that unity was ontologically prior to plurality; and this conviction led them to posit an ultimate Being in whom there was no distinction between substance and attribute, or between essence and existence—a stark, absolute unit. But, if the history of philosophy can teach us anything, it surely teaches that unity and plurality, so far from being mutually exclusive, are mutually implicatory, that the universe is an ordered whole. The monotheistic hypothesis has made a wider appeal than any other, yet it is not easy to see upon what logical grounds it can be established. If it be the case, however—as conceivably it may be—that to the intuitive insight of the mystic the central principle of reality is unveiled, it is to the painstaking study of religious experience that we must look for ultimate confirmation.

The notion of revelation, indeed, is not merely compatible with, it is implicitly involved in, the theistic hypothesis; for the notion of a Deity who remains aloof from and indifferent to the strivings of humanity would be scarcely credible. It is, as we have seen, a thoroughly rationalistic conception, for revelation is addressed by an intelligence to intelligences, and, to have any meaning, it must be intelligible. Historically it is intimately associated with the great monotheistic religions; yet logically it is compatible with polytheism, and the careful reader of Plato can scarcely fail to be impressed by the numerous references to the possibility of a divinely originated teaching. Empirical investigation of the rival claims of the various candidates for the status of a revealed religion gives no support, however, to the theory of an infallible revelation. If it take place, revelation works through human intelligences which are not exempt from error. Indeed it seems inevitable that it should do so, for the impartation of a teaching, however rational in itself, which was too advanced for the human mind to take in would obviously be futile. The notable advance in ethical insight which the history of Hebrew prophecy reveals may well have been stimulated by divine grace, yet the intuitive capacity which grasped the principles involved was an attribute of human reason. Indeed reason itself, as

Descartes clearly saw, is essentially intuitive; and every rational process is constituted by a chain of intuitions held together in memory. From the jurisdiction of reason, then, there is no escape. "Reason," in Locke's words, "must be our last judge and guide in every thing."[26]

. To the rationalist who is a religious man, however, this is not a source of despair but of elation. In the exercise of his rational powers he becomes aware of his kinship with the whole. Reason itself takes on for him a mystical significance. Philosophy and religion blend together, for, at bottom, they are identical. The rationalist is a citizen of the cosmos; it is his native country. And, as he reviews the history of metaphysical speculation, it will appear to his eyes like the path of Professor Toynbee's chariot which, mounted upon the revolving wheels of rising and falling civilizations, moves ever forward over heights and depressions, never permanently diverted from its onward course.

[26] *Essay*, Bk. IV, chap. xix, sec. 14.

INDEX